# CELEBRA
# CHRIST'S V

The Alcuin Liturgy Guides address both practical and theoretical questions concerning the practice of worship, its setting and celebration. The Alcuin Liturgy Guides (ALG) are occasional publications alternating with major liturgical studies in a series known as the Alcuin Collections.

The first two Alcuin Liturgy Guides, *Memorial Services* by Donald Gray, and *Art and Worship* by Anne Dawtry and Christopher Irvine, were published by SPCK in 2002. ALG 3, *Celebrating the Eucharist*, by Benjamin Gordon-Taylor and Simon Jones, was published in 2005, and ALG 4, *The Use of Symbols in Worship*, edited by Christopher Irvine, was published in 2007. A complementary volume to this one (ALG 5), *Celebrating Christ's Appearing*, was published in 2008. The series editor is the Revd Canon Christopher Irvine.

Members of the Alcuin Club receive free copies of the Collections, the Liturgy Guides, and the Joint Liturgical Studies. Founded in 1897, the Alcuin Club seeks to promote the study of Christian liturgy in general, with special reference to worship in the Anglican Communion in particular. The chairman of the Alcuin Club is the Revd Canon Dr Donald Gray CBE, and details regarding membership, the annual subscription and lists of publications can be obtained from the Secretary, Mr Jack Ryding, 'Ty Nant', 6 Parc Bach, Trefnant, Denbighshire LL16 4YE.

Visit the Alcuin Club website at **www.alcuinclub.org.uk**

# CELEBRATING CHRIST'S VICTORY

*Ash Wednesday to Trinity*

BENJAMIN GORDON-TAYLOR
and
SIMON JONES

Alcuin Liturgy Guides 6

First published in Great Britain in 2009

Society for Promoting Christian Knowledge
36 Causton Street
London SW1P 4ST

*British Library Cataloguing-in-Publication Data*
A catalogue record for this book is available from the British Library

ISBN 978–0–281–05979–9

1 3 5 7 9 10 8 6 4 2

Typeset by Kenneth Burnley, Wirral, Cheshire
Printed in Great Britain by Ashford Colour Press

Produced on paper from sustainable forests

# Contents

# Preface

*Celebrating Christ's Victory* is the companion volume to ALG 5, *Celebrating Christ's Appearing*, and completes our survey of the liturgical year, again with particular emphasis on the material in *Common Worship: Times and Seasons*. It should be read in conjunction with ALG 5, particularly Chapter 1 in that volume, a general introduction to the whole year, its calendar, liturgical colours and processions; and Chapter 7 in ALG 5, which deals with daily prayer and initiation throughout the year, although we have added to this in more detail in the present volume where we have thought it necessary. This present guide covers the period from the beginning of Lent through Holy Week and Easter to Trinity, but also includes some comment on the Trinity to All Saints period, including Trinity Sunday and Corpus Christi. All Saints itself is dealt with in ALG 5. In the final chapter we make brief comment on the material in *Times and Seasons* for 'Seasons and festivals of the agricultural year'. We have placed most emphasis on the major liturgies, as *Times and Seasons* itself does. As ever, we are enormously grateful for the assistance we have received from colleagues, students and friends, and hope that these two latest volumes will be of service.

B.G-T.
S.M.J.

# Abbreviations

ALG 3      Benjamin Gordon-Taylor and Simon Jones, *Celebrating the Eucharist*, Alcuin Liturgy Guides 3.

ALG 4      Christopher Irvine (ed.), *The Use of Symbols in Worship*, Alcuin Liturgy Guides 4.

ALG 5      Benjamin Gordon-Taylor and Simon Jones, *Celebrating Christ's Appearing*, Alcuin Liturgy Guides 5.

ASB      *The Alternative Service Book 1980.*

BCP      The Book of Common Prayer 1662.

CCW1      Paul Bradshaw (ed.), *Companion to Common Worship* Vol. 1, Alcuin Club Collections 78.

CCW2      Paul Bradshaw (ed.), *Companion to Common Worship* Vol. 2, Alcuin Club Collections 81.

CF      *Common Worship: Festivals.*

CI      *Common Worship: Christian Initiation.*

CP      *Common Praise.*

CW      *Common Worship.*

CWMV      *Common Worship: Services and Prayers for the Church of England* [ = Common Worship 'Main Volume'].

| | |
|---|---|
| DEL | *Common Worship: Daily Eucharistic Lectionary.* |
| DP | *Common Worship: Daily Prayer.* |
| EH | *The English Hymnal.* |
| GIRM | *General Instruction of the Roman Missal.* |
| ICEL | The International Commission on English in the Liturgy. |
| LHWE | *Lent, Holy Week, Easter: Services and Prayers.* |
| MWB | *The Methodist Worship Book.* |
| NEH | *The New English Hymnal.* |
| PE | *Common Worship: President's Edition.* |
| PS | *Common Worship: Pastoral Services.* |
| RC | Roman Catholic. |
| SM | *The Sunday Missal.* |
| TS | *Common Worship: Times and Seasons.* |
| WM | *The Weekday Missal.* |

# 1

# Lent

And now we give you thanks
because you give us the spirit of discipline,
that we may triumph over evil and grow in grace,
as we prepare to celebrate the paschal mystery
with mind and heart renewed.

(Short preface for Lent, TS: p. 218)

## Liturgical character

Whereas Advent has preparation as its primary focus, of which penitence is nevertheless a proper part, Lent has penitence as its chief purpose, yet with preparation for baptism or the renewal of baptismal vows at Easter as key positive components by ancient tradition. There is a certain gravity to Lent that Advent lacks, and yet there is also a thread of joy and expectation without which Lent would not be adequately or most profitably observed. This said, it is a season with its own unique liturgical obligations and opportunities. The cross is emphatically present from the very beginning of the season, the impact of which ought quite properly to be significant in its relative suddenness. In years where Candlemas occurs only a matter of days before Ash Wednesday, this hinge point in the liturgical year will be especially apparent; where there is a longer period of Ordinary Time before Lent, care must be taken not to allow the shadow of the cross which falls across the Presentation of Christ in the Temple to be obscured, while at the same time not giving it a liturgical emphasis which is inappropriately anticipatory of Ash Wednesday. The collects and lectionary for this part of Ordinary Time help ensure that the balance is maintained, and careful liturgical preaching will also assist.

The meaning of the title 'Lent' being 'spring' (albeit indirectly – strictly from *lencten*, thus referring to the lengthening of days in

1

spring), it must not be forgotten that there is a dimension of celebration about the season as well as of what might sound like a more sober 'observance'. George Herbert could write, 'Welcome deare feast of Lent', and it is indeed a positive time of repentance and renewal; the vision is to the cross and beyond, to the hope of new life signalled by the resurrection that each Lenten Sunday celebrates. Accordingly the liturgy needs to take this into account.

## The church and the sanctuary in Lent

The visual impact of the beginning of Lent is critical, and care needs to be taken with the appearance of the interior of the church building and the sanctuary area. TS follows the line established in ASB that 'hangings' are to be removed. This can be interpreted at least as the (temporary) taking down of colourful banners. Where a church possesses a permanent set of depictions of the Stations of the Cross, in Lent especially these ought not to be overpowered visually by other, moveable items or images, and where possible attention should be paid to their accessibility for the purposes of devotion during the season, ideally ensuring a processional way around them. Hangings and other textiles which are normally the colour of the season must of course be either removed or changed. Purple or violet is the colour of Lent in many churches (and see below for the use of rose colour on the Fourth Sunday), but in view of the need to underline the distinction between Advent and Lent and to give the season its proper integrity, as TS comments, 'this should be different from the imperial purple used for Advent' (TS: p. 222). This is less of a concern where, for example, blue is used in Advent. Indeed, ancient English custom is followed in many places in Lent by avoiding any shade of purple altogether and instead using 'Lent array', usually made of unbleached linen, and often simply decorated with embroidered images of the instruments of the passion. The impact of this is very powerful.

Careful consideration needs to be given to music in Lent. The use of the organ ought on the whole to be subdued, but need not be omitted altogether, except perhaps on Ash Wednesday.

It is again customary not to place floral arrangements in church during Lent, following the logic of the removal of hangings and the need for simplicity. TS suggests dry flowers may be used. Whatever is decided, the sanctuary and altar ought to be free of any flowers. Where, outside Lent, an altar normally has two candles at one end and a floral arrangement at the other, in Lent the flowers may be replaced by a suitable crucifix, or the candles placed at each end.

## The calendar in Lent

During Lent the observance of the season takes precedence over all but one or two festivals and the principal feast of the Annunciation which themselves, it can be argued, ought to be celebrated with a degree of restraint. Nothing may displace a Sunday in Lent (nor a Sunday in Eastertide, q.v.). Care should be taken when using the CW calendar to decide which lesser festivals or commemorations will be observed, and the balance ought to tip in favour of the enhancement of the season. This said, there are feasts of saints which only ever fall in Lent, so an informed decision needs to be made in the context of the overall celebration of Lent. It may be, for example, that the life or writings of a particular holy man or woman have a character or content germane to the Lenten context. On weekdays at the Eucharist the readings should normally be those for Lent, even where there is a lesser festival or commemoration, which may be marked by a proper collect. Even then, there is something to be said for using the Lenten Collect exclusively, and observing the saint by inclusion or allusion in the intercessions.

Where a festival falls in Lent, it may not be observed on a Sunday in Lent, but is transferred to the nearest available weekday, which may not, however, be in Holy Week or Easter Week, in which case the festival must be transferred to the nearest free weekday in the second week of the Easter season. The aim is to preserve the integrity of the Sundays of the seasons and the days of Holy Week, the Triduum and Easter Week without interruption (see TS: pp. 24–30).

## The Eucharist in Lent

The celebration of the Eucharist in Lent, for which TS provides the usual directory of seasonal material (pp. 212–20), needs to be characterized by simplicity and solemnity, without excluding the fact that, as always, in the Lenten season the Church gives thanks for and celebrates in a mystery the death and resurrection of Christ. On

Sundays the ceremonial may be simplified in order to refocus the attention, as the president's words of introduction on Ash Wednesday put it, on 'the call to repentance and the assurance of forgiveness proclaimed in the gospel', and the particular Lenten disciplines of 'self-examination and repentance . . . prayer, fasting, and self denial . . . reading and meditating on God's holy word' (TS: p. 223).

As in other seasons, many communities find it valuable to produce a special booklet for the Eucharist in Lent, in order to make rich but structured use of the available material from various sources. This need not mean a wholesale reinvention of 'what we do on Sundays', but ought to reflect careful thought and planning before Ash Wednesday arrives.

It is customary to refrain from using the word 'Alleluia' anywhere in the liturgy during Lent, until it 'returns' at the Easter Liturgy. This includes its use in hymns and Gospel acclamations (see below for alternatives).

The eucharistic vestments should be of simple design, either Lenten purple material or unbleached linen. In the absence of 'folded chasubles' *Ritual Notes* (1956: p. 26) enjoined the wearing of alb and stole by the deacon, but *no* dalmatic. This corresponds with what was said on this matter in ALG 5 about vestments in Advent (ALG 5: p. 26). Thus in Lent consideration should also be given to the deacon wearing alb and stole only for the sake of visual simplicity, and any assisting priests or concelebrants similarly vested, unless there happen to be matching purple or unbleached linen chasubles. White vestments should not be worn *except* at the Chrism Mass, the Eucharist of Maundy Thursday evening, and where a festival or principal feast (e.g. the Annunciation) occurs on a Lenten weekday.

## The Gathering

The entry of the ministers may take place as described in ALG 3, or this part of the rite might be modified in the direction of simplicity at the Principal Eucharist on a Sunday. For example, the entrance hymn could be omitted, the ministers instead entering in silence, moving to their places and sitting for a while in silent corporate preparation with the assembly, until the president stands (and all stand) to begin the liturgy.

Another possibility (which may perhaps also be used at other times of the year), admittedly less simple but nonetheless effective, is the use of a version of the traditional office of preparation, included in the Appendix to BCP 1928 as 'A Devotion before the celebration of Holy Communion', and associated especially with a High Mass, but once often used in the sacristy or in procession to the altar before a weekday celebration of the Eucharist. BCP 1928 rightly omits the prayers of confession for the presiding priest and other ministers included in the original Latin version: these would detract from the corporate penitence now usual within Western eucharistic rites. The recitation of Psalm 43 forms the core, and this might be used in a contemporary rendering, for example that in DP (p. 710), making use also of its accompanying prayer (DP: p. 711). The ministers enter and kneel before the altar. The congregation kneel, and after a few moments of silence the form begins as follows:

| | |
|---|---|
| *President* | I will go to the altar of God. |
| *All* | **To the God of my joy and gladness.** |

| | |
|---|---|
| *President* | Give judgement for me, O God, and defend my cause against an ungodly people: deliver me from the deceitful and the wicked. |
| *All* | **For you are the God of my refuge; why have you cast me from you, and why go I so heavily, while the enemy oppresses me?** |

| | |
|---|---|
| *President* | O send out your light and your truth, that they may lead me: and bring me to your holy hill and to your dwelling. |
| *All* | **That I may go to the altar of God, to the God of my joy and gladness; and on the lyre I will give thanks to you, O God my God.** |

| | |
|---|---|
| *President* | Why are you so full of heaviness, O my soul, and why are you so disquieted within me? |
| *All* | **O put your trust in God; for I will yet give him thanks, who is the help of my countenance, and my God.** |

| | |
|---|---|
| *President* | I will go to the altar of God. |
| *All* | **To the God of my joy and gladness.** |

Then either:

| | |
|---|---|
| *President* | Come, creator Spirit, light and truth; |
| | bring us to the altar of life |
| | and renew our joy and gladness |
| | in Jesus Christ our Lord. |
| *All* | **Amen.** |

| | |
|---|---|
| *Or:* | The Collect for Purity (said by all). |

The president and ministers then stand (and all stand with them), move to their places, the president first reverencing (and perhaps censing) the altar, and the Eucharist begins as usual with the greeting. The preparation text addresses God, so the liturgical greeting of the people must still be used. If the psalm prayer is used (with its note of joy), the Collect for Purity should not also be used after the greeting since the psalm prayer has already invoked the Spirit. However, as indicated above, the psalm prayer could appropriately be replaced by the Collect for Purity, incidentally restoring the latter to its original position in the Sarum Rite as part of the preparation before the Eucharist begins.

The form of the penitential rite in Lent might usefully follow a pattern which distinguishes it from that used in Ordinary Time and/or other seasons. This can be achieved partly through regular and varying use of the three possible invitations to confession in TS (p. 212), which may also be replaced by words of the president's own. As to the confession itself, TS provides three alternatives (p. 213), which should not be regarded as exhaustive. Local composition is to be encouraged, perhaps using the lections for the day to supply direct quotations or allusions. Or, some words of the BCP confession for Matins and Evensong can be used to create an effective text:

| | |
|---|---|
| *President* | We have erred, and strayed from your ways like lost sheep: |
| | Lord, have mercy. |
| *All* | **Lord, have mercy.** |

| *President* | We have followed too much the devices and desires of our own hearts: |
| | Christ, have mercy. |
| *All* | **Christ, have mercy.** |

| *President* | We have left undone those things which we ought to have done; and we have done those things which we ought not to have done; and there is no health in us. |
| | Lord, have mercy. |
| *All* | **Lord, have mercy.** |

On Sundays a congregational prayer could instead be used: the same text on all the Sundays of Lent, which can be printed in a Lenten service booklet. The alternative default text in CW Order One (CWMV: p. 169) is one possibility.

Also possible as an introduction to the penitential rite during Lent are the Summary of the Law (CWMV: p. 268) or the Commandments (CWMV: pp. 269–71).

*Gloria in Excelsis* is not sung or said at the Eucharist in Lent, except where a festival or principal feast is celebrated on a weekday, for example the Annunciation.

There is a long-standing custom, following the BCP instruction, of repeating the Collect of Ash Wednesday after the Collect of the Day at every service. However, its repetition detracts from the focus and liturgical purpose of the Collect of the Day (see ALG 3: pp. 38–9) which should far preferably stand alone, particularly on Sundays. Alternatively, the suggestion in CW that it be used as an unvarying post-Communion prayer can be taken up, but at the cost of losing the varying prayers for each week of Lent. It may also be used as a conclusion to the intercessions on any day.

## The Liturgy of the Word

Even where the full lectionary provision of three readings and a psalm is not used at other times of the year, serious consideration should be given to doing so during Lent, given the particular emphasis on the Word in the Ash Wednesday introductory text. As an alternative to the psalm or any gradual hymn, verses from the Lent

Prose could be used on each Sunday of Lent (text and melody in, for example, NEH 507).

The Gospel acclamation must not include the word 'Alleluia'. Instead a phrase such as that suggested in TS is to be used: 'Praise to you, O Christ, King of eternal glory', repeated by the congregation and again after the scripture verse. TS gives four examples of Lenten acclamations (TS: p. 214), also included in the CW *Daily Eucharistic Lectionary* edited by Simon Kershaw (DEL: p. 815). Others, together with alternative responses, will be found in Griffiths, *Celebrating the Christian Year* (Griffiths 2005: vol. 2), the RC *Sunday Missal* and *Weekday Missal* (e.g. 'Glory and praise to you, O Christ'), Young, *Enriching the Liturgy* (e.g. 'Praise and honour to Christ Jesus') and elsewhere.

Sermons at the Sunday Eucharist in Lent should follow the unfolding drama conveyed by the lectionary. A thematic sermon series would be entirely appropriate for Sunday evenings in Lent. A useful resource for the Sunday and weekday readings for the season is Irwin, *Lent: A Guide to the Eucharist and Hours* (Irwin 1985), which follows the Roman lectionary provision, especially useful for weekday introductions to the liturgy and for intercessions.

TS gives two suggested forms of intercession (pp. 215–17); if local composition is the norm (and it is to be encouraged), then these may form the basis of it. While penitence is the overarching theme of the season, the needs of the world and causes for thanksgiving should continue to be included in the intercessions in Lent.

## The Liturgy of the Sacrament

If the Peace is given here, there is an unvarying form to introduce it given by TS (p. 217), but this is another opportunity for local composition. In Lent the decision could be taken to defer the Peace until the alternative position following the Lord's Prayer, perhaps in conjunction with the option of using the Prayer of Humble Access immediately before the distribution.

Prayers at the Preparation of the Table additional to those provided in TS (p. 217) can be found in the resources given above for the Liturgy of the Word. The more general examples in CWMV are also available – of these, no. 11, 'Look upon us in mercy not in judgement . . .' (CWMV: p. 293) is especially appropriate.

It would be entirely legitimate to decide to use only one or two of the Eucharistic Prayers in Lent. Use of the extended preface (TS: p. 218) restricts the choice to A, B or E in any case; a sensible combination would be B (with extended preface) and C, with its particular emphasis on the passion, with a short preface (TS: p. 218).

Post-Communion prayers said by the president alone are those for the season in CWMV or the Collect of Ash Wednesday used as a post-Communion prayer. One of the corporate prayers given in CWMV may follow or replace the presidential text, or the Collect of Ash Wednesday could be used as a corporate prayer.

The Sundays of Lent would be appropriate occasions on which to use the solemn form of blessing (TS: p. 219).

## Ash Wednesday

The first day of a liturgical season can easily, and understandably enough, become a showcase for liturgical forms that have been dormant for up to a year, but at the beginning of Lent a certain restraint is both necessary and appropriate. It *is* very important clearly to mark the change, and suggestions have already been made as to how the arrangement of the church and the sanctuary may reflect this. In the Anglican tradition there has perhaps arisen an inchoate sense that penitence requires more words, but this is partly because visual elements of the liturgy in general have taken time to become acceptable once more. The liturgy of Ash Wednesday should strike a particular balance between spoken text, visual symbol and silence. As Perham and Stevenson note, 'Where there are too many words, the first thing to go is silence' (Perham and Stevenson 1986: p. 29); this should not be allowed to happen on Ash Wednesday, but neither should this be taken to mean that children are not welcome at the liturgy. Liturgical silence indicates a disposition on the part of the worshippers that in practice needs to allow for the possibility of unavoidable noise from infants and young children, the welcoming of whom is at all times paramount.

It has become quite usual for the principal celebration of the Eucharist on Ash Wednesday to take place in the evening. This makes pastoral sense in that it allows the greatest number of people of all ages to be present, but equally it need not prevent an earlier celebration in the morning. Where there are two or more celebrations, the imposition of ashes should take place at each. Elliott implies that ashes blessed at the first Eucharist of the day may be used at later services and even 'outside the time of Mass to meet the needs of the faithful' (Elliott 2002: p. 94). Be this as it may, the complete rite of blessing and imposition should be celebrated at the principal Eucharist of Ash Wednesday. It may be to state the obvious that it is infinitely preferable for the imposition of ashes to take place on Ash Wednesday itself, but where local pastoral circumstances compel, the liturgy provided in TS 'where necessary . . . may be used up to the First Sunday of Lent' (TS: p. 222, note 2), but not after this day.

If the BCP is used for a Eucharist on Ash Wednesday, perhaps at a service earlier in the day, the material for the ashing could be inserted from TS or, to preserve the linguistic character, adapted from sources such as *The English Missal* (*English Missal* 2002). If the strict BCP order for Holy Communion is followed, the ashes might be blessed immediately after the Prayer for the Church Militant, and imposed after the invitation to confession when all are bidden to be 'meekly kneeling upon your knees'. The prayer of confession, the absolution and comfortable words follow. If numbers are small enough to permit all to continue kneeling at the altar rail until after the Communion, this would be preferable and would eliminate two separate approaches to the altar, in the spirit of the combined invitation ('Ye that do truly . . .') to be penitent *and* 'to take this Holy Sacrament to your comfort'.

The distinctive and unique feature of the liturgy of the day at whatever time it takes place is the marking of a cross of ash on the forehead of each person as a reminder of mortality and as a sign of repentance, following the biblical tradition of ashes covering the head in mourning. It follows that the use of this symbol should be visible and reverent. The ash is traditionally obtained by burning the blessed palm or willow branches of the previous year's Palm Sunday liturgy. It is curious that at least one firm of ecclesiastical suppliers sells explicitly flameproof palm crosses, which would make obtaining ash from them rather difficult! It is true nevertheless that even theoretically combustible crosses can be hard to ignite and burn. One suggestion, to be performed with care, is to heat the palms in a saucepan until they are brittle enough to be ignited, which part of the process should take place out of doors or in a grate. An alternative relates to the use of branches of local trees on Palm Sunday (see p. 32) instead of palms – this custom is followed in some churches, often using pussy-willow (in Germany, branches of box are common). If some of these have been preserved and have had a year to dry out thoroughly, the production of ash will present no difficulty. The ash should be ground to a fine powder using a pestle and mortar, and may also be mixed with water to form a paste. This should be placed in a liturgically appropriate vessel (for example a metal or stone bowl, but not a ciborium or chalice) which should be placed on a table or stool prominently in the sanctuary (or at its entrance) before (but not on) the altar, leaving room for the celebrant to face the people when blessing it. Ashes should be imposed by the president, assisted if necessary by other ministers and lay people. There will need to be another person to impose ash on the president, and who may share in the subsequent ashing of all present. The most appropriate posture to adopt in order to receive the ash is that of kneeling, as for Holy Communion (see below), but in the case of the president and the one who imposes the ash it may be necessary to stand in order that the imposition is visible to the congregation.

A bowl of water and a towel should be provided on the credence table for the president and other ministers to wash their fingers when the imposition of ashes is complete.

The liturgy of Ash Wednesday is given a fully worked out treatment in TS (pp. 221–35), each section of which is discussed below.

## The Gathering

Consideration may on this occasion be given to omitting the usual entrance procession, instead beginning with all seated in their places, having entered when ready informally but reverently, for a period of silent prayer before the president stands for the greeting.

The president's introduction in TS (p. 223) is intended succinctly to convey the character of the season and the particular occasion, although it would not be inappropriate for the president to introduce the liturgy in his or her own words if desired. The *Trisagion* (in English) is inserted at this point in TS, but another chant or song of a penitential nature may be used. This need not automatically be assumed to be the *Kyrie eleison*. The Lent Prose is a possibility

(NEH 507). There is no penitential rite in this position since it will take place later in the form of the imposition of ashes after the sermon or (if there is no sermon) after the Gospel. While TS allows the Collect of Ash Wednesday to be replaced by the CW additional collect for the day (TS: p. 224), this would be at the cost of the fine language and imagery of the longer prayer, although there is an appropriate directness about the shorter prayer ('our lives are laid open before you').

## The Liturgy of the Word

The full provision of readings and psalmody should ideally be used, and a sermon preached. There is a case to be made for omitting the sermon on the grounds that the rite as a whole 'speaks' profoundly and scripturally in itself, but even a short homily would be an opportunity to orient the assembly liturgically and spiritually for the season.

## The Liturgy of Penitence

Two forms of self-examination and confession are given by TS (pp. 226–9), but these may be replaced by 'another suitable form'. An alternative may be found in *The Methodist Worship Book*, where the text is a more succinct form of the first TS form:

*President*   Let us pray.

*All*          **Holy and merciful God,**
               **we confess to you,**
               **and to one another,**
               **in communion with all the saints**
               **that we have sinned through our own fault**
               **in thought, and word and deed;**
               **in what we have done**
               **and in what we have failed to do.**

               **We have not loved you with all our heart, soul, mind**
               **    and strength.**
               **We have not loved our neighbours as ourselves.**

> We have not loved one another as Christ has loved us.
> We have not forgiven others as we have been forgiven.
> We have grieved your Holy Spirit.

*President*  Lord, have mercy.
*All*  **Christ, have mercy.**

*President*  We confess to you, O God, all our past unfaithfulness:
the pride, hypocrisy and impatience of our lives,
our self-indulgence and our exploitation of other people.

Lord, have mercy.
*All*  **Christ, have mercy.**

*President*  We confess our preoccupation with worldly goods and
comforts,
and our envy of others.

Lord, have mercy.
*All*  **Christ, have mercy.**

*President*  We confess our blindness to human need and suffering,
our indifference to injustice and cruelty,
our misuse and pollution of creation,
and our lack of concern for the generations to come.

Lord, have mercy.
*All*  **Christ, have mercy.**

(MWB: pp. 145–6)

The modern Roman rite assumes the self-examination and confession to have occurred privately according to the discipline of the Roman Catholic Church, and so has only a relatively brief 'Blessing and Giving of Ashes' after the homily (SM: p. 166). TS does not allow the self-examination and confession to be omitted from the public rite, although note 4 (TS: p. 222) states that 'other authorized forms of confession and absolution may replace the forms used in this service'. Indeed, whichever form of self-examination and confession is used, as indicated by the rubrics on pp. 227 and 229, if the imposition of ashes is not to follow it must be concluded with an authorized absolution, texts of which are given in CWMV (pp. 135–7, 279).

Both TS forms of self-examination and confession specifically require silence to be kept before the final corporate prayer of confession, and note 3 emphasizes that 'The silence during the Liturgy of Penitence is an integral part of the rite and should not be omitted or reduced to a mere pause' (TS: p. 222). Silence should therefore be incorporated into any alternative form that is used.

The invitation to have the ashes imposed is followed immediately by the blessing of the ashes (TS: p. 230), which may be accompanied by the sprinkling (and perhaps also the censing of them – if incense is used here, the thurifer will need to have prepared the thurible, including putting on incense, after its use at the Gospel). The prayer over the ashes may be accompanied by the sign of the cross at the words 'grant that these ashes . . .'. TS assumes that the form of words given will be used, but it may be argued that a suitable alternative could be substituted if desired. A modified text might read:

| | |
|---|---|
| *President* | God our Father, |
| | you create us from the dust of the earth: |
| | + *bless these ashes, that they may be for us* |
| | a sign of our penitence |
| | and a symbol of our mortality; |
| | for it is by your grace alone |
| | that we receive eternal life |
| | in Jesus Christ our Saviour. |
| *All* | **Amen.** |

The president should receive the ashes first from another minister as an appropriate visible example to be followed, like the president's receiving Communion first at the Eucharist. It is preferable that the whole undivided formula be used for each person, unless the ash is imposed in silence. Note 6 suggests the further alternative that 'brief personal prayer may be offered' (TS: p. 222).

TS suggests that unless silence is kept during the imposition 'a hymn, anthem or psalm may be sung' (TS: p. 230). However, there is a strong case for saying that other than the spoken formula (if used) there should be silence during the imposition, one place where the visual symbol needs to be stark and uninterrupted. Those receiving the ashes may come forward exactly as for the reception of Holy Communion, preferably kneeling at the altar rail, or they may receive the ashes standing, one by one, from the ministers who stand on the sanctuary step.

When all have received the ashes, and one of the concluding prayers (TS: p. 230) has been said, the ministers wash their fingers (for which a lavabo bowl and towel need to be to hand, ideally brought by a server) and return either to their places or to the table where the ash is placed, for the Peace. Ideally this table should be left in place as a reminder of its part in the liturgy as a whole, but if for reasons of space or the practicalities of administering Holy Communion it needs to be removed, then this should be done now or during the offertory hymn.

## The Liturgy of the Sacrament

Unique to Ash Wednesday in TS are the prayers at the preparation of the table (TS: p. 231), which reflect the particular penitential character of the day. TS does not provide a proper preface for Ash Wednesday only. Instead, as noted above, three short prefaces and one extended preface are provided for use on any day of the season until the Fifth Sunday of Lent. On Ash Wednesday itself, however, TS recommends and reproduces the extended preface (TS: p. 232). This text recalls the president's words of introduction to the Ash Wednesday liturgy which concern the disposition of the Church and the individual throughout the season. While the extended preface is to be preferred, TS allows one of the short prefaces as an alternative (TS: p. 232).

A special introduction to the Lord's Prayer ('Lord Jesus, remember us in your kingdom and teach us to pray') is given by TS (p. 232), a form which could suitably be used on any occasion throughout the year.

Either or both the presidential Prayer after Communion and the corporate text may be used (TS: p. 233).

## The Dismissal

TS provides a short responsory and a Dismissal Gospel for optional use before the blessing (see ALG 5: p. 31 and CCW2: pp. 54–5 for comment on the latter as a genre). The solemn form of blessing (TS: p. 235) is to be preferred on this Greater Holy Day. After the usual words of dismissal, it would be appropriate for the president and other ministers, and then the congregation, to leave in silence.

## The Fourth Sunday of Lent

The Fourth Sunday of Lent, in the Latin tradition *Laetare* ('Rejoice', the first word of the Latin introit) Sunday, is the Lenten counterpart of the Third Sunday of Advent, *Gaudete* (see ALG 5: p. 25). It has a note of heightened joy sometimes marked by the use of rose colour vestments. In England it has also come to be known as Mothering Sunday by elision with a secular custom which itself was suggested by the lighter feel of the day in the liturgical tradition (as noted by the TS Introduction to the Season, p. 211). Many parishes and other communities therefore choose to make thanksgiving for mother-hood a key focus of the Principal Service on this day. The CW lectionary provides alternative readings for this purpose, one or more of which may be chosen in place of the Lenten ones. By doing so in the case of the Gospel it must be remembered that the very brief Mothering Sunday alternatives are in place of substantial Lenten Gospels, for example the story of the prodigal son in Year C. The liturgical emphasis chosen is a matter for careful pastoral local deci-sion – it is possible to achieve a satisfactory balance. In some places a Marian flavour is chosen in accordance with the theme of mother-hood; this should not be taken to be effectively an opportunity for an additional feast of Our Lady, but on the other hand the example of Mary is of obvious importance to the theme. TS does not provide any specific resources for Mothering Sunday – an alternative collect and post-Communion are given in CWMV (p. 49) – but it is a clear opportunity to involve children in the liturgy, for example in the blessing and presenting of flowers to the mothers present.

## Penitential services in Lent

The season provides a good opportunity for the use of the provision for 'A Corporate Service of Penitence' and the considerable accom-panying resources in CI (pp. 228–64). The material may be used, for example, on a Sunday evening in Lent, and may be imaginatively combined with the Eucharist, using also the TS seasonal material, in which case the Peace, Preparation of the Gifts and Eucharistic Prayer should follow the Absolution (CI: p. 228, note 4).

## The Way of the Cross

In his *Parson's Handbook*, Percy Dearmer touches very briefly on the Stations of the Cross and dismisses them immediately since he believes them to have 'no authority' in the Church of England and to give 'undue prominence to one part of our Lord's life and work' (Dearmer 1932: p. 32). Dearmer's suspicion of this devotion has been shared by many Anglicans, and, indeed, it is only relatively recently that the celebration of the Way of the Cross by Anglicans from a range of traditions, and, indeed, by other Christians who are not Roman Catholics, has become more widespread. There are, perhaps, a number of reasons for this. There is now a greater appreciation of the origins of this devotion which had been considered by some to be no more than medieval superstition. The experience of many modern-day pilgrims to Jerusalem resonates with that of the earliest Christian visitors who, on reaching the Holy City, wished to retrace the steps of Jesus on his journey to Calvary and then, back at home, sought to re-enact this journey liturgically so that they could 'engage actively with the path of suffering walked by Jesus' (TS: p. 236). The travel diary of the Spanish (or, possibly, French) nun Egeria provides evidence of a Good Friday procession from the Mount of Olives to the Church of the Holy Sepulchre from as early as the end of the fourth century (Wilkinson 1999: pp. 135–6).

In the fourteenth century, tableaux depicting the events associated with each holy place were erected by the Franciscans, who had responsibility for the sites, and used as part of the devotion. The decision to fix the number of stations at 14 was not taken until 1731, when Pope Clement XII combined nine scriptural and five non-scriptural events (see Table 1.1). Although this form remains that most commonly used today, with their use strongly encouraged by Elliott (Elliott 2002: p. 124), in 1991 Pope John Paul II introduced a new sequence of scriptural stations. The presence of non-scriptural events in the traditional form undoubtedly added to the suspicion with which they were viewed by some Christians, and discouraged their use outside the Roman Catholic Church. With the exception of the (optional) fifteenth station of the resurrection, the Way of the Cross provided in TS is identical to the 1991 sequence of John Paul II although, not surprisingly, it is not attributed to him! Sixteen years later, the same form was approved for meditation and public celebration by Benedict XVI, and celebrated by him at the Colosseum on Good Friday, 2007. (An English translation of the meditations used on that occasion, written by Mgr Gianfranco Ravasi, can be found on the Vatican website, <www.vatican.va>)

Table 1.1   Comparing 'traditional' and 'scriptural' Stations of the Cross

Non-scriptural stations are indicated in italics.

| | |
|---|---|
| 1  Pilate condemns Jesus to death | Jesus in agony in the garden of Gethsemane |
| 2  Jesus accepts his cross | Jesus betrayed by Judas and arrested |
| 3  *Jesus falls the first time* | Jesus condemned by the Sanhedrin |
| 4  *Jesus meets his mother* | Peter denies Jesus |
| 5  Simon helps Jesus carry the cross | Jesus judged by Pilate |
| 6  *Veronica offers her veil to Jesus* | Jesus scourged and crowned with thorns |
| 7  *Jesus falls the second time* | Jesus carries the cross |
| 8  Jesus speaks to the women of Jerusalem | Simon of Cyrene helps Jesus to carry the cross |
| 9  *Jesus falls the third time* | Jesus meets the women of Jerusalem |
| 10  Jesus is stripped of his garments | Jesus is crucified |
| 11  Jesus is nailed to the cross | Jesus promises the kingdom to the penitent thief |
| 12  Jesus dies on the cross | Jesus on the cross; his mother and his friend |
| 13  Jesus is taken down from the cross | Jesus dies on the cross |
| 14  Jesus is placed in the tomb | Jesus is laid in the tomb |
| (15)  (Jesus risen from the dead) | (Jesus risen from the dead) |

As the introduction to the rite makes clear, TS does not provide liturgical resources for the traditional sequence. Most parishes which already have stations around the walls of the church are likely to have the traditional tableaux and wish to retain this sequence when they celebrate the Way of the Cross. Indeed, if these are a prominent feature within the church building, it would seem strange to ignore them in favour of another pattern. There are many publications which contain excellent material, including meditations, for use with the 'traditional' stations, but there is also something to be said for communities and individuals devising their own reflections and for the use of extempore prayer.

Those who do not already have tableaux around the walls of their places of worship should not be discouraged from using this service. There are a number of other options, with which the community can be encouraged to engage creatively. Before considering some of them, there are a couple of *caveats* which are perhaps worth mentioning. The Way of the Cross is a rite which, wherever possible, should be celebrated on the move, so that worshippers can have a sense of praying as they walk in the steps of Jesus. For this reason, although the projection of images on to a fixed screen would be one way of providing visual input into the service, it would inevitably require the rite to be a static celebration. Similarly, simply to display the numerals 1 to 14 at intervals around the church provides a processional route but no visual stimulus to prayer, unless images are included in an order of service.

As TS points out, images of the stations are readily available, and these may be displayed around the church. TS also makes suggestions for creative, symbolic representations of each station: 'the Agony in the Garden could be represented by a goblet or chalice with wine in it, the betrayal and arrest by a pair of handcuffs etc.' (TS: p. 237). The task of devising these could be assigned to various groups within a parish. For example, Lent and home groups, candidates for baptism or confirmation, a youth group, the Mothers' Union, members of the choir, the local ministry team, servers, the Sunday school, etc. Richard Giles encourages communities to devise their own stations, of whatever number, 'provided that they bring alive ... the stages of Christ's long lonely journey to his death' (Giles 2008: p. 81). Stations which contain contemporary images and which reflect the shared experience of the worshipping community can have an undoubted power and poignancy. In creating them it is important not to forget that the primary purpose of including any such representations is to assist the worshippers in making connections between the world in which they live and the Christ whose cross has redeemed it and them. Whatever their style or design, the stations should not obscure the message of the cross, but enable the Christian to be drawn more deeply into its saving mystery.

The celebration of the Way of the Cross is by no means restricted to Lent and Passiontide but, in most communities, this is when it is most likely to be celebrated. Its use, like the manner of its celebration, is flexible, and may be used corporately or by individuals. As TS suggests, it is not necessary for all the stations to be used in one act of worship (TS: p. 237). If extended meditations on each one are included, it may be appropriate to restrict the number to three or four within a single service, framed by the Gathering and Conclusion. Alternatively, an address may be given as part of the Gathering (before the collect) or before the Conclusion. In churches where eucharistic devotions and Benediction form part of the regular pattern of worship (see Chapter 5), this may appropriately replace the Conclusion.

The Way of the Cross is also ideally suited for use with children. In many churches this is included within their pattern of worship on Good Friday. The second volume of Gill Ambrose's *Together for a Season* offers a number of creative ideas as to how this might be done (Ambrose 2007: pp. 70–84).

Stations may also form the Liturgy of the Word within a celebration of the Eucharist. In this context, so as not to unbalance the rite, it is probably best not to use all the stations within the same service; but if the service is celebrated weekly during Lent, it should be possible to cover them all within the season. TS gives guidance as to how such a liturgy should be ordered and also points to the rubrics relating to A Service of the Word with a Celebration of Holy Communion (CWMV: p. 25). Since every station is, in some sense, penitential, it seems unnecessary to include an extended penitential rite as part of the Gathering. One possibility would be for the president's words of introduction to lead into a period of reflective silence followed by a *Kyrie* Confession and a simple Prayer for Forgiveness, such as:

| | |
|---|---|
| *President* | May almighty God, |
| | who sent his Son into the world to save sinners, |
| | bring us his pardon and peace, now and for ever. |
| *All* | **Amen.** |

(CWMV: p. 135)

The whole rite could be structured as in Table 1.2:

Table 1.2   Structure of the rite for the Way of the Cross

| *CW Order One (2000)* | *Way of the Cross (2005)* |
|---|---|
| **The Gathering** | |
| Trinitarian Invocation | |
| Greeting | |
| | Sentences |
| | Introduction |
| *Kyrie* Confession (TS: p. 213 or p. 260) | |
| Prayer for Forgiveness | |
| Collect | |
| **Liturgy of the Word** | |
| | Stations of the Cross |
| **Liturgy of the Sacrament** | |
| Peace (TS: p. 265) | |
| Offertory | |
| Eucharistic Prayer | |
| Lord's Prayer | |
| Breaking of the Bread (alternative form, CWMV: p.179) | |
| Giving of Communion | |
| Prayer after Communion (the prayer for Palm Sunday, CWMV: p. 397, is appropriate) | |
| **Dismissal** | |
| | Responsory |
| | Blessing |
| Dismissal | |

TS encourages the use of the fifteenth station of resurrection, particularly outside Lent and Passiontide (TS: p. 236). Having spent some time meditating on the passion and death of Christ, to conclude with just one station of the resurrection does seem rather abrupt, as Elliott suggests (Elliott 2002: p. 124). That said, if the Blessed Sacrament is exposed at the end of the service, the unity of the death and resurrection of Christ is proclaimed, and the congregation departs with the blessing of the risen Lord, who revealed himself to his disciples in the breaking of the bread (Luke 24.35).

Although it may often be appropriate for a priest or deacon to officiate at the Way of the Cross, there is no requirement for an ordained minister to preside. If the officiant is ordained, a cotta or surplice and purple or red stole may be worn and, if desired, a cope. (Within the context of the Eucharist, the president should wear a chasuble throughout.) Whoever presides, that person should lead the Gathering and Conclusion, but the readings and devotions at individual stations may be led by others, including members of the congregation. Unless they have been warned about this in advance, this is usually only possible if they are given a full text to read. Two candles should be lit on the principal altar (or, if the Gathering and Conclusion are led from a side chapel, on that altar), and a crucifer and acolytes may lead the procession.

## The Gathering

To assist the congregation to prepare for the liturgy in silence, no music should be played before the service, and any preparations carried out before people arrive. If there is a Calvary in the church, a bowl of incense may be placed there, and people encouraged to light candles in front of the Calvary as they arrive and leave. TS suggests that a large cross be carried into the church at the beginning of the service (TS: p. 237). This should again be done in silence. The minister stands before the altar, or in another central place, to introduce the rite. TS concludes the Gathering and every station with the *Trisagion*, which should be sung, wherever possible. While this text is certainly appropriate and bears repetition, some variation may be appropriate. Other texts traditionally used in this position include the Lord's Prayer (omitting the doxology), the Hail Mary and the *Gloria Patri*. Whatever is chosen, a limited number of texts that can be recited by heart is better than a constantly changing refrain.

## Stations

After the first congregational prayer, a verse or verses of a hymn may be sung as the procession moves to the first station. If a large cross is used, this should lead the people. Although it may be carried by the crucifer for the whole service, members of the congregation could also take turns in carrying it. Careful consideration needs to be given to what music is sung between the stations. Traditionally, verses of the *Stabat Mater* (NEH 97) are used. Since some may be uncomfortable with its Marian emphasis and each half-verse may be too short to cover the movement from one station to another (unless the whole hymn is sung twice), one or two verses from a selection of well-known Lenten and Passiontide hymns may be preferred. An example of this may be found in *The Walsingham Pilgrim Manual*.

Each station begins with a versicle and response. With the exception of the crucifer and acolytes, it is appropriate for everyone to genuflect or make a profound bow while this is said. It is also customary for each station to be announced before the response is made. So, for example:

*Officiant/Reader* The fourth station: Peter denies Jesus.
We adore you, O Christ . . .

Even if the officiant leads the meditation at every station, others can take it in turns to read the biblical passages which, in TS, are printed in full. At the thirteenth station, 'Jesus dies on the cross', an extended period of silence may be preferred to a spoken reflection. At each station, the officiant/reader should face the station for the response and closing prayer, and turn to the congregation for the scripture reading and reflection/meditation.

## Conclusion

After the last station, the officiant and congregation return to the place where the service began. TS suggests that the Conclusion should begin with some form of response, followed by the Lord's

Prayer and a collect. After this, a choice of two responsories is given before the officiant says the final prayer. Elliott refers to the Roman custom of the priest taking a wooden cross and blessing the people with it at the end of the service (Elliott 2002: p. 66). If a large wooden cross has led the procession round the stations, this could be used for the blessing, if it is not too heavy. If its weight makes this impossible, the priest may hold on to it with the left hand while blessing with the right. If the priest does bless the people at the end of the service, the following form would be preferable to the one given in the rite:

*Priest*     Christ give you grace to grow in holiness,
to deny yourselves, take up your cross, and follow him;
and the blessing . . .

(TS: p. 219)

After the blessing, the ministers and people may leave in silence or, if a more confident expression of the triumph of the cross is required, 'Lift high the cross' or another suitable hymn may be sung.

# 2

# Passiontide and Holy Week

And now we give you thanks
because, for our salvation,
he was obedient even to death on the cross.
The tree of shame was made the tree of glory;
and where life was lost, there life has been restored.
(Short preface for Passiontide, TS: p. 266)

## Liturgical character

'Passiontide' is an English term derived from the Latin *passio* meaning 'suffering'. Beginning on what is commonly referred to as Passion Sunday, the Fifth Sunday of Lent, and continuing through Holy Week until Holy Saturday, during this fortnight the Church's Lenten observance grows in intensity as the liturgical focus gradually shifts to Calvary and the final events of Jesus' earthly life. Although the CW calendar (TS: p. 9) and DP (p. xix) clearly indicate that Passiontide begins on the Fifth Sunday of Lent (or, to be more precise, at Evening Prayer the day before), what TS describes as the 'Introduction to the Season' focuses entirely on Holy Week (see CCW2: p. 83) with no reference to the previous week. Such inconsistency may reflect the change in Roman Catholic practice in 1969 when, as a result of the reforms of the Second Vatican Council, Passiontide was suppressed (although a Preface of the Passion was still used during the fifth week of Lent) and Palm Sunday, being the Sunday when the Passion Gospel is proclaimed, was renamed Passion Sunday. This calendrical revision has not been adopted by the Church of England, nor is it strictly correct to refer to Passiontide as a season, since it is part of Lent.

That said, TS contains excellent 'seasonal' material (TS: pp. 260–7) which may appropriately be used in these two weeks, where no other provision is made. No Principal Feast, Festival, Lesser Festival or Commemoration may be observed in Holy Week (for a table of transferences of Principal Feasts and Festivals, see TS: p. 30; see also ALG 5: pp. 11–16). In the week following Passion Sunday these may be observed, though so as not to detract from the thematic focus of this period it would be appropriate only to mention Lesser Festivals and Commemorations in the intercessions, rather than using a proper collect and readings.

More churches than would normally have a daily celebration of the Eucharist will do so on the Monday, Tuesday and Wednesday of Holy Week. The CW Principal Service Lectionary provides three readings and a psalm for each day, in addition to the office lectionary (see below). In a week which contains such a rich liturgical diet, particular care needs to be taken not to overload these liturgies: one reading and the psalm in addition to the Gospel may be considered sufficient, particularly if a homily is to be preached, and the Creed is not said. Silence plays a very important part during the liturgies of Holy Week. To give these celebrations a more contemplative feel, extended periods of silence may be kept after the homily (or Gospel reading), during the prayers and after Communion. Alongside these, even though in most churches weekday Eucharists will be said rather than sung, it may be considered appropriate to introduce some music into the service, perhaps by singing a simple, unaccompanied Gospel acclamation, a response during the prayers and a hymn at the offertory.

Although Dearmer argues strongly for the use of red (in honour of the precious blood) in Passiontide (Dearmer 1932: pp. 113, 452), CW suggests that the same liturgical colour that has been used in Lent (either purple or Lent array) should also be used on Passion Sunday and in the week following. On Palm Sunday and for the liturgy on Good Friday, red vestments are worn; white is the colour for the Chrism Eucharist and the Eucharist of the Last Supper on Maundy Thursday; and on the Monday, Tuesday and Wednesday of Holy Week, red (CW) or purple (RC) may be used.

The reforms of Vatican II also removed the universal obligation for Roman Catholic churches to cover crosses, statues and other devotional images with purple veils during Passiontide. Although it is now left up to individual episcopal conferences to decide whether it should be practised, Elliott clearly favours it:

The custom of veiling crosses and images in these last two weeks of Lent has much to commend it in terms of religious psychology, because it helps us to concentrate on the great essentials of Christ's work of Redemption.

(Elliot 2002: p. 67)

During Passiontide the church becomes the stage on which the Christian community performs the drama of salvation, not as passive spectators of a passion play, but as active participants whose lives are touched and transformed by its saving grace. Such participation is similar to that which Cyril of Jerusalem describes in his second homily to the newly baptized:

What a strange and astonishing situation! We did not really die, we were not really buried, we did not really hang from a cross and rise again. Our imitation was symbolic, but our salvation a reality.

(Yarnold 1994: p. 78)

As the Lenten pilgrimage nears its final destination, images draped in purple express the community's grief at the death of its Saviour. By obscuring images of the crucified one and his cross, the community's desire to experience afresh the reality of Christ's salvation is intensified. Even if this custom isn't followed, purple cloth may be draped round the arms of the principal cross in the church, and replaced by a white cloth, symbolizing the grave-clothes, at Easter. If unbleached linen is preferred to purple during Lent, then the passion veils should also be of this colour. On Palm Sunday, palm branches may be attached to the processional cross, whether or not it is veiled. If banners have remained in church during Lent, they should be removed during Passiontide and, as *Ritual Notes* suggests, simpler candlesticks may be used on the altar (*Ritual Notes* 1946 [1894]: p. 143).

## Daily Prayer

ALG 5 makes some suggestions as to how the office may be celebrated during this period (p. 98). The omission of the *Gloria Patri* at the end of the psalms and canticles is no longer required, though DP suggests it for the Triduum (DP: p. 20). In 2005, when the General Synod authorized the new weekday lectionary (GS 1520A), the opportunity was taken to make some minor alterations to the Holy Week provision in the CWMV (pp. 554–6). The amended version, which now appears in the annual almanacs, is as in Table 2.1:

Table 2.1    Readings for daily prayer

|  | *Morning Service* | *Evening Service* |
| --- | --- | --- |
| Monday of Holy Week | Psalm 41<br>Lamentations 1.1–12a<br>Luke 22.1–23 | Psalm 25<br>Lamentations 2.8–19<br>Colossians 1.18–23 |
| Tuesday of Holy Week | Psalm 27<br>Lamentations 3.1–18<br>Luke 22.[24–38] 39–53 | Psalm 55.13–24<br>Lamentations 3.40–51<br>Galatians 6.11–end |
| Wednesday of Holy Week | Psalm 102*<br>Wisdom 1.16–2.1;<br>2.12–22<br>or Jeremiah 11.18–20<br>Luke 22.54–end | Psalm 88<br>Isaiah 63.1–9<br><br>Revelation 14.18–15.4 |
| Maundy Thursday | Psalms 42, 43<br>Leviticus 16.2–24<br>Luke 23.1–25 | Psalm 39<br>Exodus 11<br>Ephesians 2.11–18 |
| Good Friday | Psalm 69<br>Genesis 22.1–18<br><br>A part of John 18–19<br>if not used at the<br>Principal Service<br>or Hebrews 10.1–10 | Psalms 130, 143<br>Lamentations<br>5.15–end<br>John 19.38–end<br>or Colossians 1.18–23 |

Peculiar to Holy Week are the offices of Tenebrae (from the Latin for 'darkness'), special anticipated forms of Matins and Lauds for Maundy Thursday, Good Friday and Holy Saturday which are celebrated in semi-darkness on the preceding evenings. Tenebrae was part of the official liturgy of the Roman Catholic Church until the reform of the Holy Week rites by Pius XII in 1955, and has recently undergone something of a revival, not least in some Anglican circles. Elliott gives detailed instructions on how the old rite might be celebrated today (based on Fortescue and O'Connell 1948: pp. 275–8), and also how the modern Roman Office of Readings and Morning Prayer might be accompanied by traditional Tenebrae ceremonial (Elliott 2002: pp. 208–14).

Although there is no provision for Tenebrae in TS or DP, a number of modern Anglican forms are available, the most accessible being that contained in The Episcopal Church's *Book of Occasional Services* (2004: pp. 74–92). The characteristic features of Tenebrae are the chanting of verses from the Lamentations of Jeremiah (in which a letter from the Hebrew alphabet introduces each verse) and the gradual extinguishing of candles after each psalm and canticle is sung. The large triangular candlestick used for Tenebrae is known as a hearse and is traditionally set up in front of the altar on the south side of the sanctuary. If the full form of the office is used, 15 candles, traditionally unbleached, are required. The altar candles should also be lit and, again, unbleached candles used, if possible. The altar candles are extinguished during the *Benedictus*. If the altar has six, these should be extinguished one at a time during each of the last six verses of the canticle. If the altar has two, they may be extinguished during the last two verses. After the *Benedictus*, it is customary for the last candle on the hearse to be hidden beneath or behind the altar rather than being extinguished. At the end of the office a sudden noise (Latin *strepitus*) is made, symbolizing the earthquake at the crucifixion. This effect can be achieved in various ways – by slamming a book closed, banging something against the side of a pew or stall, or dropping a heavy object on the floor. After this the hidden candle is returned to its position at the top of the hearse, signifying the dawning light of the resurrection.

In its full form the service consists of 15 psalms and canticles, the *Benedictus*, nine readings and nine responsories. Although a daunting prospect for many Christian communities, the office has the potential for creative flexibility in its performance and can be celebrated in a number of ways depending on the musical resources available. Where there is a strong choral tradition, some of the great polyphonic settings of the Lamentations readings may be sung. When there is no choir, members of the congregation may take it in turns to read the psalms, or they can be said antiphonally. If it is desired to shorten the service, the *Book of Occasional Services* suggests an abbreviated form which reduces the number of psalms and readings by half so that only a seven-branch candlestick is required (p. 92). Recognizing that most churches will not possess a Tenebrae hearse, the appropriate number of candles or lamps can be arranged in a tray of sand, in triangular form in front of the altar, or in another prominent place. Apart from the extinguishing of candles and the *strepitus*, there is no other ceremonial associated with this service. The officiant may wear a cassock and cotta and be assisted by a server.

More popular than Tenebrae is the night office of Compline. This service is part of the Holy Week provision in a number of churches, sometimes combined with an address. If there is to be a homily, this should be given before Compline is said, so that the congregation can depart in silence at the end of the service. There is no requirement for altar candles to be lit, but depending on the layout of the church building and the size of the congregation, it may be appropriate for the people to gather around a Calvary to pray the office (in which case it would be better for a purple cloth to be draped over the arms of the cross rather than for it to be fully veiled), or for a large cross to be placed on the floor in front of the altar. Lamps may be placed on it, as in the Taizé tradition, either before the service starts, or by members of the congregation during the prayers.

DP gives propers for Passiontide (p. 352) which may replace equivalent texts in the standard order (pp. 337–43). The CWMV also provides an order in traditional language (pp. 89–98). The officiant may wear a cassock and cotta, or simply a cassock. If possible, some of the service should be sung, preferably unaccompanied. The RSCM has published two booklets providing useful musical resources: one which includes the modern texts set to traditional tones (*Music for Common Worship VI: Night Prayer (Compline)*: 2005) and an edition by the Plainsong and Medieval Music Society of the traditional language form (*Compline: An Order for Night Prayer in Traditional Language*: 2005). If musical resources are limited, the psalms may be said and the *Nunc dimittis* sung to a metrical version, such as 'Faithful vigil ended' (NEH 44). Whether texts are said or sung, Night Prayer should be prayed quietly, with generous silences after the reading and during the prayers.

# Palm Sunday

TS provides a complete liturgy (pp. 268–77) which incorporates the two distinctive and customary elements of Palm Sunday: the procession of palms and the reading or singing of the Passion narrative. There is now relative flexibility as to the precise texts and choreography, reflected in TS and the resources of other churches, although the principal elements must retain appropriate emphasis.

## Preparations

The decoration of the church should reflect both the continuing days of Passiontide and the specific character of Palm Sunday. It is very appropriate, therefore, to incorporate branches of palm, yew, box or willow. The latter three reflect northern European custom in that in the past palm, not being indigenous, was often difficult to obtain, and so locally available alternatives were used. This is important as an example of the inculturation of the liturgy that is hardly noticed. Indeed, the scriptural account itself does not specify palm – 'others cut branches from the trees and spread them on the road' (Matthew 21.8) – but in a Middle Eastern context it is highly likely. Luke, of course, has no branches at all, only 'cloaks' (Luke 19.36). The point is not just the geographical accuracy, but what the use of the branches symbolizes – the kingship of Christ, the irony of the royal procession that will soon be repeated in grotesque mockery as the royally dressed Christ is taunted, tortured and made to 'process' to the throne of Calvary. Some Western European paintings of Christ's entry into Jerusalem show people climbing trees and busily cutting down branches as Christ passes – yet more irony in that they are too late to 'straw them in the way' (as the King James version has it), so inexorable is Christ's journey to his passion, death and resurrection. Something of this is present in George Herbert's poem 'Easter':

> I got me flowers to straw thy way;
> I got me boughs off many a tree:
> But thou wast up by break of day,
> And brought'st thy sweets along with thee.
> (Herbert 1995: p. 39)

Therefore for the procession of palms, while the small palm crosses readily available from ecclesiastical suppliers may of course be conveniently used, so might actual branches of indigenous trees, most traditionally in England willow, but as already stated, branches of evergreens are also appropriate. People can be encouraged to bring a branch with them from their garden to carry in the procession – this also connects the celebration of the liturgy to the homes of the community, and represents an offering of each person. However, there should always be palm crosses available for those for whom this is not possible, for taking to those unable to be present as a blessed token of the liturgy celebrated, and to ensure that there is a supply from which ash can be produced for use on Ash Wednesday the following year. There would seem to be no objection, though, to this ash being obtained through the burning of *any* branch which was used on Palm Sunday.

The branches may be used to decorate the altar cross and the processional cross. The liturgical colour for Palm Sunday is red. The president may wear a cope for the procession, or a chasuble for the entire rite, particularly if the church does not possess a red cope.

## The Commemoration of the Lord's Entry into Jerusalem

The general remarks about liturgical processions in ALG 5 (pp. 19–21) should be referred to in addition to the following specific comment. As TS encourages (note 1: p. 268), ideally the liturgy of Palm Sunday should begin in a place apart from the church, in order to be able to process to it. Often this will be a church hall or nearby school, but the procession may well be presented as a greater act of witness to the local community if it begins in a public place in a town centre, perhaps at a market cross or at the symbolic centre of the community, for example the Town Hall, or in a shopping centre. If the procession will involve a significant distance along public roads, for safety's sake the advice and assistance of the police must be sought in advance, and in any case the procession should be carefully marshalled, particularly since it will, hopefully, include children.

An alternative place at which to gather is the churchyard cross, where there is one. In medieval times this cross featured prominently in the Palm Sunday liturgy: the procession left the church and customarily made a 'station' at the cross before returning to the church.

Many Palm Sunday processions now include a live donkey, where one is available. This is to be welcomed, although the obvious needs and consequences of such an animal need to be kept in mind.

If it is truly not possible to gather in a place apart from the church, the Commemoration of the Lord's Entry into Jerusalem must still be made, 'at a convenient place' (TS: p. 268), the procession taking place either wholly within the church or within and without, 'all or some of the congregation taking part, as circumstances permit' (TS: p. 268).

At the gathering-place, thought must be given to where the liturgical ministers are to stand in relation to the people – this will to some extent depend on the nature of the place, but visibility and audibility must be most importantly considered. The president and the reader of the Palm Gospel should realize how inaudible an unamplified human voice can be out of doors unless actually shouting. If the crowd is very large, the possibility of an unobtrusive amplification system should be considered.

The liturgical ministers should themselves carry palms or branches unless they are carrying something else (for example, the thurible). Some churches possess a set of especially large palm branches for the sacred ministers to use each year – large to serve as a substantial visual symbol rather than to indicate hierarchy. One of the other ministers or a server will need to hold the president's branch or palm during the Greeting and Introduction so that the hands are free. The Gospeller should hold a palm while proclaiming the Gospel, but will need to hand it to a server while signing and censing the book.

When all have gathered, the liturgy begins with the traditional text 'Hosanna to the Son of David', preferably sung, in one of the two forms given in TS (p. 269), There are several choral versions (for example by Orlando Gibbons), plainchant and more contemporary settings, some including the prophecy of Zechariah, given here as an extended alternative employing the 'Hosanna' as the antiphon. The president then greets the people using the 'Grace, mercy and peace . . .' formula (which may be preceded by 'In the name of the Father . . .') and introduces the liturgy (TS: p. 270). The introduction can use 'other appropriate words', but the text supplied is a succinct statement of the nature of the Palm Sunday liturgy. There are very similar alternatives in the MWB (p. 237), and the modern Roman rite (SM: p. 201).

The prayer which follows is to be said by the president with hands extended as all hold up their palms or branches (TS: p. 270). It may be made more obviously a prayer of blessing by its modification as follows:

*President*     God our Saviour,
               whose Son Jesus Christ entered Jerusalem as Messiah
                   to suffer and to die;
               + *bless these palms, that they may be* for us signs of
                   his victory,
               and grant that we who bear them in his name . . .

The people and their branches may be sprinkled (and possibly censed) after the prayer. The Palm Gospel follows (there are three alternatives as given in the CW Principal Service lectionary) with the usual announcement and conclusion. Incense may be used. After the Palm Gospel the president may put on incense for the procession.

The procession is begun by the minister who has read the Gospel or the president saying, 'Let us go forth, praising Jesus our Messiah' (TS: p. 271). The order of the procession should typically be: thurifer, acolytes and crucifer, choir, other servers, MC, ministers, deacon (or Gospeller in priest's orders), president, people.

During the procession the hymn 'All glory, laud and honour' is traditionally sung, although another suitable hymn may be substituted. If the processional route is long, more hymns may in any case be required. Depending on the length, a typical choice would be 'All glory, laud and honour' for the outdoor stage of the procession, and 'Ride on, ride on in majesty' on entering the church (accompanied by the organ). It often happens that during the outdoor procession the singing becomes rather ragged – the choir should give a strong lead, and if a brass band is available it would make an important contribution. It may be wise for those leading the procession to stop at the door of the church for the rest to catch up, so that all may regroup for the final stage into church. Indeed, this may be made into a formal station by halting to sing or say, for example, the antiphon

O Jerusalem, look towards the east and behold:
    lift up your eyes, O Jerusalem, and behold the power of
    your King!

at the door, when all have gathered around. When all are ready, the procession continues into the church, singing a hymn, and all go to their places. The ministers reverence and the president censes the altar, after which the cope is exchanged for a chasuble if the latter is not already worn. The collect follows. The president will need to hand over the palm carried in the procession so as to leave the hands free.

## The Liturgy of the Word

At least one reading must now precede the Gospel – it may be felt that the total length of the liturgy suggests only one reading at this point, especially since the focus of the Liturgy of the Word is the Passion narrative. The traditional text for the Passion on Palm Sunday is that of Matthew, but the CW Lectionary has Matthew in Year A, Mark in Year B and Luke in Year C, in accordance with the three-year cycle. While the full Passion reading is preferable, it could be shortened for local pastoral reasons – suggested abbreviations are given in the CW Lectionary. The Passion reading offers opportunities for creative participation: at its simplest it may be read by one person alone; there are versions available in dramatic form, for example CW *Proclaiming the Passion*, which permit the involvement of a number of people, either taking individual roles or as part of a 'crowd' ('Crucify him!'), the latter part perhaps taken by the whole congregation; visual drama may be incorporated into the reading; or the Passion may be sung by three persons (originally three deacons) according to the traditional chant, perhaps with choir participation, if local resources and abilities allow. Above all, however, and whichever option is chosen, there must be a sense of the drama of the unfolding Passion narrative in which all participate by their presence and attention, whether or not they have a particular role. It is customary for all to stand for the whole narrative, although those who are unable to do so should not feel embarrassed to sit. At the words 'breathed his last' all genuflect or kneel for a space (or alternatively bow the head).

The precise choreography will depend on which option is chosen, how many people are involved and the layout of the church, but obvious concerns will be audibility and visibility. This is an opportunity for the creative use of the entire space. For example, the narrator (Evangelist) could be at the lectern, the person reading the part of Jesus (not necessarily the president) at the altar, other individuals in the pulpit and in the aisles, the crowd to one side in a transept or side chapel – there are many possibilities to explore. Rehearsal for the Passion is essential, particularly where large numbers of 'actors' are involved, but equally all should be prepared to move quickly on from any mistakes so as not to allow the momentum to be lost.

The Passion reading may be heralded with an acclamation (TS: p. 272) or a hymn. The different manner of announcing and concluding the Passion should be noted – there are no congregational responses. Incense is not used, nor lights carried. The thurifer must ensure that the thurible is ready for the Preparation of the Gifts, but preferably should not do so during the Passion narrative, to which all should attend; it may be done during the intercessions.

TS implies that a sermon is mandatory. Strictly this is indeed the case, but it can be argued that the Passion drama may on this occasion speak for itself.

The Prayers of Intercession after the sermon (TS: pp. 272–3) are from the examples in the seasonal resources for Passiontide (TS: pp. 261–5), and may be adapted or replaced by local composition.

### The Liturgy of the Sacrament

From the sermon onwards the liturgy of Palm Sunday proceeds almost entirely in the same way as a normal Sunday Sung Eucharist, with appropriate texts. The suggested words of distribution are the 'broken for you . . . shed for you' alternative from CWMV (p. 295). The CW post-Communion (or 'other suitable prayer') is followed by an optional congregational text (TS: p. 276), here unique to Palm Sunday.

### The Dismissal

The blessing may be either the solemn seasonal form or 'another suitable blessing' (TS: p. 277), which could be the short blessing ('Christ crucified draw you to himself . . .') from the Passiontide provision (TS: p. 267). The Dismissal is in the standard CW form. There is no option of a Dismissal Gospel.

At the end of the liturgy, people should be encouraged to take a palm cross for anyone they know who was unable to be present in person.

## The Chrism Eucharist

Whether celebrated on Maundy Thursday or on another day in Holy Week, the Chrism Eucharist is now a well-established diocesan occasion, normally celebrated in the cathedral and combining the blessing of oils with the renewal of commitment to ministry. Historically, the latter is a relatively recent development, introduced by Paul VI as part of the liturgical reforms in the Roman Catholic Church in the middle of the last century. In the Church of England, where this act of renewal has, in a number of dioceses, been extended to include all authorized ministries, it is the blessing of oils which has proved more controversial. As recently as 1982 a form for the blessing of oils was rejected by General Synod, with one member describing the Liturgical Commission's proposals as 'rather like a form of white magic' (General Synod Proceedings 1982: p. 349). As noted in ALG 4, given the extensive, albeit optional use of oil in the rites of CW, it is hard to believe that the Church of England has come so far in such a relatively short period of time (ALG 4: p. 56).

TS provides a number of resources for the celebration of a Chrism Eucharist, together with an historical introduction and some simple rubrics. How the rite is celebrated will depend very much on local circumstances, not least when and where the service takes place, the musical resources available and who attends. Sadly, in many dioceses the Chrism Eucharist is considered to be a rite for clergy (and, perhaps, other authorized ministers), rather than an important celebration for the whole Church, and so it is rarely advertised in local communities. The fact that, for many, the renewal of commitment to ministry is seen to be more important than the blessing of oils has not helped in this respect. Wherever possible, the bishop should encourage lay representation from every Christian community in the diocese of which he has oversight, and not just by those who are Readers or members of local ministry teams. Although administered by the ordained, the holy oils which are blessed at the Chrism Eucharist are God's gift to the whole Church. If the Church of England is going to recover confidence in using them, it is vital that local communities are more widely represented on this occasion, even if this means thinking of a more convenient time for the celebration of the rite than the morning of Maundy Thursday.

As note 1 indicates (TS: p. 279) the bishop presides at the Chrism Eucharist. In some dioceses it is customary for the diocesan and assistant bishops to take it in turns to preside at this service. On this occasion, as the diocese gathers around its bishop, it is important that, wherever possible, the diocesan should preside and, to give expression to his teaching ministry, also preach.

The liturgical colour is white, the same colour that will be used for the Eucharist of the Lord's Supper, and preferably not the best white or gold that will be used at Easter. If it is the custom of the cathedral or church to veil crosses during Passiontide, the altar and processional crosses should be veiled in white, rather than purple, for this celebration. The president wears a chasuble and mitre and also carries his crosier. On this occasion, when the three orders of ordained ministry will be present, it is also appropriate for him to wear a white dalmatic under the chasuble. If other bishops are present, they may concelebrate in matching white chasubles and plain white mitres, or in alb and stole. If the Eucharist is not concelebrated, they may wear copes and plain white mitres, or alb and stole. Only the presiding bishop carries a crosier.

Priests and deacons should also be invited to robe for this service. Alb and white stole is probably the most appropriate vesture for the clergy, particularly if the Eucharist is to be concelebrated, although some will prefer surplice/cotta and stole or choir dress. While it is desirable for everyone to follow the same dress code, it is more important for the clergy of the diocese to process and sit together as a body than to worry about what they are wearing!

In the Western tradition, deacons exercise an important role at the Chrism Eucharist, carrying the three oils to the bishop to be blessed. Note 4 indicates that they may be 'vested in distinct colours: purple for the oil of the sick, green for the oil of baptism, and white for the oil of chrism' (TS: p. 279). It would thus be appropriate for the deacons of the oils to wear an alb with the appropriately coloured stole and dalmatic. When other deacons are present, one may act as the deacon of the Gospels and another as the deacon of the Eucharist. These should be vested in white stoles and dalmatics, preferably matching the bishop's vestments. If lay ministers are to join the clergy in renewing their commitment to ministry (Form A, TS: pp. 282–3), they should also be invited to robe. Readers may wear an alb, cotta, or choir dress.

The oils should be prepared before the service and contained in three large vessels so that their contents are clearly visible to the congregation. The distribution of the blessed oils at the end of the service is often a messy and lengthy business, particularly if large numbers of clergy are present. If this is thought to be problematic, the custom practised in some cathedrals may be followed, and a sufficient number of small plastic containers, clearly labelled, filled with each of the oils before the service. These may be carried on trays, behind the principal vessels, and distributed at the end of the Eucharist. As note 3 makes clear, perfume or balsam (often referred to as the oil of flowers) is customarily added to the oil used for the chrism to give it a sweet smell (TS: p. 279). A sufficient quantity needs to be added to the olive oil so that it can be clearly distinguished from the other two. This may be done before the service or during the rite itself. If small, plastic containers are used, it will need to be added to that oil before the service, but may still be added to the principal vessel during the course of the rite.

ALG 3 contains notes on the bishop as president, the role of the deacon and concelebration (pp. 12–22). In the following sections we will restrict our comments to peculiar features of the Chrism Eucharist and the texts provided in TS.

## The Gathering

TS suggests a form with which the bishop may greet the congregation, which may be prefaced by the Trinitarian invocation. The opening response from Revelation 5.10, highlighting the priestly vocation of all the baptized, is certainly appropriate, but would perhaps be better followed by the simple apostolic greeting:

| | |
|---|---|
| *Bishop* | Peace be with you |
| *All* | **and also with you.** |

The *Gloria in Excelsis* is sung at the Chrism Eucharist. Having abstained from using this canticle during Lent (apart from on Principal Feasts and Festivals) it may seem strange to sing it in Holy

Week. However, there is a strong note of praise and celebration which needs to be sounded at the beginning of this Eucharist, as the Church rejoices in the ministries with which God has blessed it, and the sacramental means by which those ministries are carried out. If there is a choir, it may sing a setting of the canticle, but if there is not, a metrical version may enable greater participation than a congregational setting which may not be familiar to everyone. If 'Glory in the highest to the God of heaven' (NEH 363) is sung, the final line of the first verse may be altered to avoid the 'alleluia' which, of course, is not part of the text of the canticle: 'Singing highest praises to our heavenly King'.

## The Liturgy of the Word

Three readings and a psalm are provided for each of the years of the lectionary. Even if clergy make up the majority of the worshippers at this service, the first two readings should be read by lay people, and preferably by those who are not robed. A deacon should read the Gospel, first seeking a blessing from the bishop. Before the sermon, it would be appropriate for the bishop, wearing the mitre, to kiss the Book of the Gospels, and then bless the people with it (GIRM: p. 175).

It has already been suggested that the bishop should exercise his teaching ministry by preaching on this occasion. Depending on the position of the bishop's chair and the layout of the building, this ministry may also be symbolized by his preaching from the chair (either standing or sitting), wearing the mitre and holding the crosier. The Creed is not said at this Eucharist.

## Renewal of Commitment to Ministry

The Renewal of Commitment to Ministry follows the sermon. Three forms are provided in TS. Form A permits ordained and lay ministers to renew their commitment together, responding to questions which relate specifically to their order or ministry. It is followed by a series of biddings, led by the bishop, which include material from the Roman rite. Form B1 is for ordained ministers only, either bishops and priests alone, or bishops with priests and deacons speaking their part together. If only bishops and priests renew their commitment, form B2 may be used for deacons immediately before the proclamation of the Gospel. Form C, based on the Methodist Covenant Service, is much shorter and does not distinguish between the three orders or between ordained and lay ministry.

Because of the strong connection which now exists between the renewal of commitment to ministry, the blessing of oils and the events of Maundy Thursday (Christ washing his disciples' feet and the institution of the Eucharist), even if the Chrism Eucharist is not celebrated on that day there is a strong argument for allowing the renewal of commitment to ministry to be for the ordained alone (using Form B) and providing a diocesan service for the celebration of lay ministry at another time in the year, perhaps near Pentecost, All Saints or Christ the King. At a time when some see a crisis of confidence in the ministry of the ordained and as, simultaneously, the Church is trying to encourage more vocations to the diaconate and priesthood, for the three orders of clergy to renew their vows together would celebrate and encourage their distinctive ministries and also permit the ecclesiological relationship between bishop and priest, which is so often ignored, to be clearly expressed.

Depending on the layout of the building and the position of those who are to participate in the act of renewal, the bishop may sit or stand at the chair or in another prominent place, wearing the mitre and holding the crosier. If he sits, in Forms A and B1 he should stand when the lay person addresses the question to the bishop(s) and remove the mitre for the biddings which follow. Those renewing their commitment stand throughout, while other members of the assembly stand for the biddings and for the Peace. If there is a deacon of the Eucharist, that person should invite the congregation to share the Peace.

## Blessing of the oils

TS gives no indication as to when the oils should be blessed. Historically, in the Western tradition the blessing of the oil of the sick took place before the end of the Eucharistic Prayer, and the blessing of the other two oils after Communion. The modern Roman rite permits the entire rite of blessing to follow the Liturgy of the Word, and the Church of England has tended to follow this practice, blessing all three oils between the Peace and the Eucharistic Prayer. An anthem or a suitable hymn, such as 'Blest by the sun, the olive tree' (NEH 512) is sung as the three oils and the gifts of bread and wine are brought to the bishop at the chair or wherever the renewal of ministry vows was led from. The oils are carried by the three deacons, with an additional person carrying the balsam, if required, and the bread and wine by lay members of the congregation. The order of the procession is as follows: oil of the sick, oil of catechumens, and oil of chrism, followed by the eucharistic elements. Although the *Ceremonial of Bishops* directs that the balsam, if used, should lead the procession, it would perhaps be equally acceptable for the person carrying that vessel, perhaps a child or someone to be baptized or confirmed at Easter, to walk alongside the deacon carrying the oil for the chrism (*Ceremonial of Bishops* 1989: p. 99). The deacon of the Eucharist may begin the preparation of the altar as the procession approaches so that, when the bishop takes the bread and wine after the blessing of the oils, all is ready for the bread to be placed on the altar and the wine poured into the principal chalice.

Each deacon announces the name of his or her oil as it is presented. For the blessing, the oil may be held in front of the bishop, who stands without mitre or crosier, or it may be presented to the bishop who may then place it on a table in front of him. If it is convenient, the priests of the diocese may stand around him, but they should not obscure the view of other members of the assembly. The bishop extends his hands to the *orans* position as he sings or says each prayer, bringing them together again as the people respond. If balsam is to be added to the oil for the chrism, this takes place after the blessing of the oil of catechumens; it is likely that a long spoon will be required to mix it. The Roman rite talks of *consecrating* rather than *blessing* the chrism, and the ceremonial for its consecration is more elaborate than that associated with the other two oils. In addition to the mixing of balsam, the bishop breathes over the oil in the form of a cross, symbolizing the invocation of the Spirit, before beginning the prayer, which is considerably longer than the other two and rich in scriptural imagery. The consecration is also concelebrated, the priests extending their right hands towards the chrism in silence when the bishop invokes the Father's blessing on the oil. Although such ritual may seem unnecessary, it does highlight the sacramental significance of the oil of chrism which is associated particularly with the gift of the Holy Spirit in rites of initiation, ordination and coronation. Referring to the distinctive character and grace of the chrism, Cyril of Jerusalem says to the newly baptized:

> Be sure not to regard the myron (chrism) merely as ointment. Just as the bread of the Eucharist after the invocation of the Holy Spirit is no longer just bread, but the body of Christ, so the holy myron after the invocation is no longer ordinary ointment but Christ's grace, which through the presence of the Holy Spirit instils his divinity into us. It is applied to your forehead and organs of sense with a symbolic meaning; the body is anointed with visible ointment, and the soul is sanctified by the holy, hidden Spirit.
>
> (Yarnold 1994: pp. 82–3)

### The Liturgy of the Sacrament

After the oils have been blessed the bishop takes the bread and wine. He may hand them to the deacon of the Eucharist or a server so that the preparation of the altar can be completed. An anthem or a hymn may be sung or, if the first five verses of 'Blest by the sun' were sung for the procession of the oils, the final verse may be sung here, followed, if necessary, by an organ improvisation. The bishop then moves to the altar for the offertory prayers and, if incense is used, to cense the gifts and the altar. The Eucharist continues in the usual way. ALG 3 makes some suggestions about the arrangement of vessels when there are a large number of communicants (pp. 25–6). TS provides a short and extended preface for the Eucharistic Prayer. In a service which has the potential to be very long, Prayer E is a good choice and allows the extended preface to be used. At the time of Communion, although it may be tempting only to involve members of the clergy in the administration of the sacrament, it is important that lay eucharistic ministers are invited to administer Communion as well.

### The Dismissal

TS provides a Trinitarian solemn blessing which may be prefaced by the greeting:

*Bishop*   The Lord be with you
*All*      **and also with you.**

The deacon of the Eucharist should give the dismissal. To honour the consecrated oils, if incense is used the thurifer may lead the procession, with the deacons carrying the oils walking behind the acolytes and crucifer.

## The Triduum

The rites of the Easter Triduum (the Eucharist of the Last Supper on Maundy Thursday, the Liturgy of Good Friday and the Easter Vigil) are the most important liturgical services in the Christian year. Through a proper celebration of these rites, the Christian community is drawn into a transforming experience of the saving events of Christ's passion, death and resurrection. Spread over three days (Triduum, from the Latin, means 'three days') these distinctive liturgies have developed from a single unitive celebration which began on the evening of Holy Saturday and ran through the night to a celebration of the Eucharist at dawn on Easter morning, a liturgy in which the whole of the Paschal Mystery was celebrated. If the rites of the Easter Triduum enact the drama of salvation, then it is helpful to consider each celebration as one part of a tripartite whole, or of the Triduum as a single performance in three acts.

There are a number of changes of scene over the course of the Triduum as the community moves from the Upper Room to Golgotha and, finally, to the garden tomb. The way in which these scene changes are liturgically enacted will vary from place to place, not least because of size and layout of the worship space and the size of the congregation for each of the celebrations. Creative use of the building is to be encouraged, particularly if seating is not fixed. For example, in some buildings it may be possible for the Eucharist of the Last Supper to be celebrated at a westward-facing altar with the community gathered round in a semi-circle. The Liturgy of the Sacrament on Good Friday could be celebrated eastward facing at the High Altar, on which the crucifix used for veneration has been placed. At the Vigil, the congregation could gather outside the church for the blessing of the new fire and lighting of the Easter Candle, sit in the nave for the Vigil of Readings, move to the font for the Liturgy of Initiation and then process to the sanctuary for the Liturgy of the Eucharist. Recognizing that, in many buildings, it will not be possible to perform so many scene changes in such a short period of time, there are nevertheless very few buildings in which some variation to the normal way of doing things is not possible during this Week of Weeks.

## The reception of holy oils during the liturgy of Maundy Thursday

As its name suggests, TS provides a simple rite for the oils blessed at the Chrism Eucharist to be received into the parish at the beginning of the Eucharist of the Last Supper (TS: p. 292). In many communities, where little is known of the liturgical use of oil, this serves to raise its profile at one of the most important celebrations of the year and to make the important link between the rite celebrated by the bishop and the ongoing sacramental ministry of the parish. Its use is therefore strongly recommended. If possible, the oils should be carried in glass jugs or cruets so that they can be easily seen. Although TS refers to three ministers carrying the oils, if the congregation has been represented at the Chrism Eucharist by a group of lay people, three of them may be invited to fulfil this role (in lay dress). Alternatively, as suggested in ALG 4, it may be appropriate for a hospital visitor or someone who has recently been absent from the worshipping community through illness to carry the oil of the sick; a candidate for baptism or a godparent to carry the oil of catechumens; and an ordinand or someone involved in preparing people for confirmation to carry the oil of chrism (ALG 4: p. 56). The oils are presented in turn and, after each, the president (the reference to the bishop in TS is an error) says a short prayer which makes useful reference to the way in which it will be used. The oils should then be taken to the place where they are reserved.

## The Liturgy of Maundy Thursday

Maundy Thursday is described by Dearmer as 'the birthday of the Eucharist' (Dearmer 1932: p. 457), and yet it is much more than that. Jewish Passover, institution of the Eucharist, washing of feet, agony, betrayal and condemnation are all commemorated on this day, whose dramatic Eucharist of the Last Supper begins in festive mood and ends in darkness and anguish, as the Christ who has celebrated his last meal with his friends goes out into the night to confront the reality of his sacrificial vocation. Giles is surely right to say that 'Maundy Thursday is . . . the supreme example in the Church's Year of liturgy as *formation*' (Giles 2008: p. 99). Feet are washed, bread is broken; on the night of the new commandment Christians are called to model their lives on the actions of the one who commands them to do these things in memory of him.

Ideally, there should be only one celebration of the Eucharist in any place of worship on Maundy Thursday (except when there is also the Chrism Eucharist), the evening celebration of the Eucharist of the Last Supper, at which the whole community gathers together. However, if there are members of the congregation who are unable to attend an evening celebration, it may be considered appropriate to celebrate a Eucharist earlier in the day (without any of the Maundy ceremonies).

Various preparations are required for the Eucharist of the Last Supper. An Altar of Repose needs to be set up in a suitable place. This is where the Watch will take place after the Eucharist and where the sacrament which will be used for Holy Communion on Good Friday will be transferred. Although some Altars of Repose are very elaborate, with many candles and flowers, they need not be so. Elliott, who believes that the place of reposition should be 'as beautiful as possible', gives some guidelines (Elliott 2002: pp. 97–8), but what is appropriate in particular communities will vary according to local custom and the design and layout both of the church and of the place where the Watch will take place. That said, wherever possible the Altar of Repose should be at some distance from the principal altar so that the transfer of the eucharistic elements can more obviously symbolize the movement from the Upper Room to Gethsemane. Elliott suggests that it need not be a 'real altar', but it should resemble one, perhaps with a tabernacle or repository for the sacrament placed centrally and surrounded by candles and flowers. Any crosses in the chapel should be removed or veiled in white. Sufficient seating should be arranged for those who watch during the night, with space for them to kneel. It is also desirable for a pricket stand or container of sand to be prepared so that people may light candles and leave them there.

Also before the Eucharist, holy water stoups are emptied and the Blessed Sacrament removed from its normal place of reservation and taken to a suitable place where it can be kept until after the

Easter Vigil. Although Elliott suggests that it may be used, if necessary, to provide additional hosts for the Liturgy of Good Friday, this
would destroy the unity of the two rites and should not be encouraged. This reserved sacrament should only be used, *in extremis*, to
give Communion to the sick and dying. In terms of setting the scene
for the celebration of the Triduum, the removal of these sacramental
elements is significant, since along with the new light of Easter they
will be restored, renewed by the power of the resurrection, during
the course of the Paschal Vigil. If it is desired to highlight the
removal of the sacrament, just before the beginning of the Eucharist
a priest or deacon may go to the aumbry or tabernacle, wearing a
humeral veil over an alb and white stole, accompanied by two
servers. One may lead the minister to the temporary place of reservation, ringing bells to highlight the presence of the sacrament. The
other may remove the sacrament lamp and any veil from the aumbry
or tabernacle. The door should be left open so that it is clear that the
sacrament is not reserved there and the lamp may be transferred to
the place of temporary reservation.

For the Eucharist itself, consideration needs to be given to whose
feet will be washed and where this will take place. If possible, all
those who wish to have their feet washed should be permitted to do
so, to give a sense of the whole congregation identifying themselves
with the disciples in the Upper Room. For many members of the
Church of England, footwashing, though now a more common phe-
nomenon since its appearance in LHWE in 1986, remains a cause of
embarrassment and so it is rare to have too many volunteers! If
numbers are small enough and there is sufficient space so that it is
possible for the whole community to gather in a semicircle around
the altar for the Eucharist, then the priest can wash the feet of
anyone who wishes to participate by moving from person to person
around the semicircle. Alternatively, if the congregation is seated in a
more traditional forward-facing formation, those who have their
feet washed can be asked to sit next to the aisles. If a group of 12
people are chosen to represent the congregation, care should be
taken to ensure that they are truly representative, including women
and men, as well as people of different ages. None of the Holy Week
liturgies are historical re-enactments, and so the Roman Catholic
insistence that, for this reason, only men should be chosen seems
unnecessary (Elliott 2002: p. 98). A large bowl, ewer of water and

towels need to be prepared before the service, as well as an amice or large towel for the president to wear around the waist. Members of the congregation should be given hand-held candles if they are to follow the Blessed Sacrament as it is carried to the Altar of Repose, and candles should also be placed ready for choir, servers and other ministers if they have nothing else to carry at that point in the service.

White is the liturgical colour for this Eucharist and, if possible, different vestments from those that will be worn at Easter should be used. The altar and processional crosses should also be veiled in white. Incense, which will not be used on Good Friday, is particularly appropriate at this Eucharist, even in churches where it is only used occasionally. The president should wear a chasuble throughout the rite, and a white humeral veil (but not a cope) may be worn for the transfer of the eucharistic elements to the Altar of Repose. At this celebration, at which the institution of the Eucharist is commemorated, if the parish is served by more than one priest, concelebration is particularly appropriate, so that all the priests who exercise a sacramental ministry within the community may give liturgical articulation to their priesthood and express their collegiality (for guidelines on concelebration, see ALG 3: pp. 15–18). If matching chasubles or stoles are not available, priests who assist/concelebrate may be encouraged to wear their ordination stoles, if they are white.

TS provides a fully worked-out order of service for the Eucharist of the Last Supper (pp. 293–304), with the following special features: the Washing of Feet follows the sermon within the Liturgy of the Word and the Conclusion includes the Stripping of the Sanctuary and the Watch.

While a number of hymns helpfully articulate many of the themes which are expressed in this liturgy, some popular eucharistic hymns, such as 'Alleluia, sing to Jesus' and 'Lord, enthroned in heavenly splendour' are not appropriate because of their use of 'alleluia', which will only return at the Vigil. Newman's 'Praise to the holiest in the height' is particularly appropriate as an entrance hymn, combining a confident ascription of praise with references to Gethsemane and Calvary. At the offertory, William Turton's 'O thou, who at thy Eucharist didst pray' seems particularly appropriate, as is the less well known 'This is the night' (CP 134), based on a text by Peter Abelard, which may be sung to R. R. Terry's fine tune 'Highwood'

(CP 28). A number of contemporary songs and chants, not least Graham Kendrick's 'The Servant King', may supplement the traditional provision, and Stephen Dean's *The Great Week* is a valuable musical resource for all the major liturgies of Holy Week.

## The Gathering

The Gathering takes place as usual. The president's greeting may be preceded by the Trinitarian invocation and, although words of introduction are optional in TS, they seem particularly appropriate on this occasion, providing an opportunity for the president to introduce not only the Eucharist of the Last Supper but also the community's observance of the Triduum. A penitential *Kyrie*, using verses from Psalm 51, is suggested and may be followed by the *Trisagion* (or the *Kyrie* if another form of confession has been used). So as not to overload this part of the rite, or to detract from the *Gloria in Excelsis* which follows (and which, in TS, should be printed in bold, p. 295), optional elements such as the *Trisagion* or *Kyrie* are probably unnecessary. As at the Chrism Eucharist, the singing of the *Gloria* on Maundy Thursday may feel somewhat out of keeping with the overall tone of the celebration, but its place is justified as a powerful reminder that, within this one liturgy, praise and thanksgiving for the institution of the Eucharist need to be sharply juxtaposed with penitence and grief for arrest and betrayal. It is customary for bells to be rung during the *Gloria* and then kept silent until the *Gloria* is sung again at the Easter Vigil. Hand-bells may be provided for clergy and some members of the congregation, and church bells may be rung, but any ringing on Maundy Thursday should not be as exuberant as that which will accompany the celebration of the resurrection. The Gathering concludes with the collect.

## The Liturgy of the Word

The readings proceed in the usual way, preferably using all three readings and the psalm. In TS the washing of feet follows the sermon (p. 298), but it is also possible to dramatize the Gospel reading by washing the feet while it is being proclaimed. This is not a re-enactment of what Jesus did in the Upper Room, but is rather the obedient response, liturgically expressed, of his present-day disciples to his command to follow his example and to serve the world as his servants.

If this option is preferred, the Gospel should be proclaimed from the same place as the other two readings (no Gospel procession is possible). When the Gospeller reaches John 13.4, '[Jesus] got up from the table, took off his outer robe, and tied a towel around himself', the president removes the chasuble and ties a large amice or towel around his or her waist. When the end of verse five is reached, the Gospeller stops reading and a suitable hymn, anthem or chant begins. TS provides a metrical form of *Ubi Caritas*. In the modern Roman rite *Ubi Caritas*, which along with other chants once accompanied the footwashing (Fortescue and O'Connell 1948: p. 287), is sung at the offertory while a collection for the poor is being taken, but it is in many ways more appropriate in this earlier position. The Taizé version of the chant would also be suitable, and Dean makes other suggestions, including the song 'A new commandment' (Dean 1992: pp. 24–31). Accompanied by another minister carrying the bowl and servers with towels, the president takes the ewer of water and moves to the first person whose feet are to be washed. The president and the other minister kneel. The president pours water over the foot into the bowl and then passes the ewer to a server in order to dry the foot with a towel. The president may kiss the foot before standing and moving to the next person.

After the first chant or song has finished, or when the footwashing is about halfway through, the president and one of the people participating in the footwashing continue the Gospel (John 13.6–11), reading the parts of Jesus and Peter:

| | |
|---|---|
| *Gospeller* | Jesus came to Simon Peter, who said to him, |
| *Peter* | Lord, are you going to wash my feet? |
| *Jesus* | You do not know now what I am doing, but later you will understand. |
| *Peter* | You will never wash my feet. |
| *Jesus* | Unless I wash you, you have no share with me. |
| *Peter* | Lord, not my feet only but also my hands and my head! |
| *Jesus* | One who has bathed does not need to wash, except for the feet, but is entirely clean. And you are clean, though not all of you. |
| *Gospeller* | For he knew who was to betray him; for this reason he said, 'Not all of you are clean.' |

The president then washes that person's foot and those of the others remaining, while a second hymn, chant or song is sung. At the end of the footwashing the Gospeller concludes the reading (John 13.12–17, 31b–35) and the president returns to the chair, removes the amice or towel and puts on the chasuble again. Elliott suggests that the president's hands should be washed before the chasuble is put on (Elliott 2002: p. 203), but this would seem to destroy the symbolism of what has just taken place and, in any case, the president's hands will be washed before the Eucharistic Prayer. At the end of the Gospel reading the president says the concluding prayer (TS: p. 298).

If the washing of feet follows the Gospel, as TS suggests, the procedure is very similar. Suitable hymns, chants and songs are sung throughout and conclude after the chasuble has been put on again. The Nicene Creed is not said on Maundy Thursday and the Eucharist continues with the Prayers of Intercession, for which TS provides a form which, regrettably, requires a different congregational response at the end of each petition, requiring the text to be printed in full in an order of service. To avoid this, the response '**Lord, graciously hear us**' may be made each time 'Lord, hear us' is said. As this form also ends rather abruptly, it would be appropriate, after the last bidding, for the intercessor to introduce a period of silence which the president could conclude with the response 'Merciful Father' or a suitable concluding prayer (see, for example, Griffiths 2005: p. 71).

## The Liturgy of the Sacrament

As already mentioned, there is a tradition of taking a collection for charity at the Eucharist of the Last Supper. Having challenged his disciples with the new commandment, this is a good way in which the community can express its desire to obey it. If *Ubi Caritas* was not sung during the washing of feet, it should be used now.

TS provides an extended responsorial acclamation at the preparation of the table (p. 300). If desired, two offertory hymns may be sung, the first while the collection is being taken and the gifts of bread and wine are brought to the altar and prepared, and the second after the prayer at the preparation of the table, while the gifts, altar, ministers and people are censed and the president's hands are washed. Alternatively, if the offertory hymn is long enough, it may be broken halfway through and the prayer at the preparation of the table said in the middle of it. However this is done, if Holy Communion is to be given on Good Friday from the elements consecrated at this Eucharist, sufficient bread (and wine) needs to be prepared. If Communion is to be given in both kinds on Good Friday (for a discussion of this see below), the wine for Good Friday should be consecrated in a cruet or flagon rather than in an additional chalice.

TS provides an extended and short preface for use during the Eucharistic Prayer (p. 301). The former has the advantage of referring to the washing of feet, the new commandment and the Last Supper, whereas the latter concentrates solely on the institution of the Eucharist. Whichever preface and Eucharistic Prayer are chosen, TS suggests that the president may insert into the institution narrative after the words 'in the same night that he was betrayed' (or equivalent) the phrase 'that is, this very night' (p. 293). No bells should be rung during the Eucharistic Prayer, and although the old Roman rite used to permit the use of clappers (Fortescue and O'Connell 1948: p. 281), their use can be rather comical. Moreover, if bells are generally rung during the Eucharistic Prayer, silence makes for a much more striking contrast.

During the administration of Communion the candles on the Altar of Repose are lit (they should not be lit before the beginning of the Eucharist) and, if a second thurible is available, this is prepared. The congregation's hand-held candles should also be lit and, if possible, some of the electric lights dimmed or turned off. At the end of Communion a ciborium (and cruet or flagon) which is large enough to contain the sacrament which will be used on Good Friday is placed on the corporal in the centre of the altar, and may be covered with a white veil and secured with a ribbon. Everything else is removed from the altar and the ablutions may be performed elsewhere, such as at the credence table.

## Transfer of the Holy Eucharist

Although TS makes no explicit reference to the transfer of the Holy Eucharist, a procession to the place where the Watch is to be kept is alluded to (p. 304). In considering how to do this, it is important to bear in mind that this liturgical act is not, strictly, a procession. It is simply the means by which the eucharistic elements are moved from the Upper Room to Gethsemane so that, as Jesus' disciples follow him out into the night, his sacramental presence may provide the focus for their watch during the silent hours of his agony. The ceremonial and the music which accompany the transfer should not, in any way, detract from this nor sound a note of triumph or victory. This is not Corpus Christi. Although Giles suggests that the sacrament may be placed in a monstrance for the 'procession', this would be entirely inappropriate (Giles 2008: p. 116).

After a period of silence the president stands for the Prayer after Communion (TS: p. 302). The congregational prayer '**Almighty God, we thank you for feeding us**' (CWMV: p. 182) is not appropriate if the congregation are being encouraged to remain and watch. The crucifer and acolytes form up as they would normally do at the end of the Eucharist, leaving enough space for the thurifer(s) and ministers to come between them and the altar. At the same time the ministers (if possible, the president assisted by two ministers, one on either side) approach the altar and genuflect. If there is sufficient space for them to kneel behind the altar, they approach from the east; if not, they stand west of the altar facing east. The president puts incense into the thurible(s) and the ministers kneel facing the altar. The president takes one of the thuribles and, after bowing with the other ministers, censes the sacrament with three double swings. They bow again and the thurible is returned to the thurifer. The thurifer(s) then move to stand east of the acolytes and crucifer. If a humeral veil is used, a server places it round the president's shoulders. As soon as this has been secured, the ministers stand and approach the altar. After genuflecting, one of the ministers gives the ciborium to the president so that it is covered by the humeral veil. The ministers then turn and move towards the Altar of Repose as the first four verses of the hymn *Pange, lingua*, 'Sing my tongue' (NEH 268), or an appropriate alternative, are sung, preferably unaccompanied.

As Elliott suggests, the Transfer of the Holy Eucharist should move at a 'slow and reverent place', led by the acolytes and crucifer (Elliott 2002: p. 210). Behind them come the choir, if there is one, any additional servers, other ministers, the thurifer(s) (it is no longer required for them to walk backwards or sideways; Fortescue and O'Connell 1948: p. 284), and the president holding the ciborium (with the two ministers walking either side, one of them carrying the flagon, if there is one). If possible, up to six servers or members of the congregation carrying candles should flank the sacrament and, in some churches, an *umbrellino* is carried above it. Other members of the congregation, carrying their hand-held candles, follow the sacrament.

When the acolytes and crucifer reach the Altar of Repose they should stand to one side leaving room for the president to get to the altar. If the chapel or space around the altar is big enough for a large number of people to gather, the choir, servers and other ministers may approach and position themselves appropriately. However, if the space is small, they may stand aside so that some of those follow-ing the sacrament may occupy the space. When the president reaches the place of reposition, the sacrament is placed on a corporal in the centre of the altar. The ministers genuflect, then kneel in front of the sacrament, and a server removes the humeral veil. If possible, others gathered round should also kneel. '*Tantum ergo*', 'Therefore we, before him bending', the last two verses of *Pange, lingua*, may be sung. Towards the end of the penultimate verse, a thurifer approaches and the president stands to put on more incense. Kneeling again, the president censes the sacrament, as before, with three double swings. If the sacrament is to be locked in a tabernacle or aumbry, one of the ministers, or the president, stands, goes to the altar, places the sacra-ment in the place of reposition, genuflects and locks the door. Return-ing to kneel in front of the altar, all pray in silence for a while. After at least a minute's silent adoration, the ministers (and any servers who are kneeling) stand, genuflect and return to the sacristy to prepare for the stripping of the sanctuary. The acolytes may leave their torches either side of the altar and the thurible(s) may also be left nearby. Some of the congregation may wish to remain at the Altar of Repose during the stripping; others may prefer to return to the nave. If there is a choir, they need not return to stalls in the chancel, if that is where they usually sing from, but may move to another suitable place in the church, preferably at the back, for the stripping.

## Stripping of the sanctuary

The formal part of the Liturgy of Maundy Thursday concludes with the stripping of the sanctuary. There is no set order for this, but it may be helpful to assign particular tasks to individual ministers and servers before the Eucharist begins. It should be carried out as simply and unhurriedly as possible, with the minimum of fuss. The ministers should remove their vestments and, if desired, the president (and deacon) may put on purple stoles. If possible, the altar cross and candlesticks, frontal and altar linen, sanctuary lamps and bells should be removed from the church, leaving the sanctuary as bare as possible. These should also be removed from other parts of the church, except for the Altar of Repose. The old English custom of washing stone altars with water and wine is continued in some places (*Ritual Notes* 1946 [1894]: p. 155).

TS suggests that Psalm 88 may be used during the stripping or verses from the Lamentations of Jeremiah (p. 303). Psalms 22 and 51 are also appropriate on this occasion. If musical resources permit, these should be sung, but the organ should not be used. The simplicity of unaccompanied plainsong is particularly effective. Alternatively the psalmody may be said, or the stripping may take place in silence. Where possible, lights in the sanctuary and nave should be gradually dimmed or switched off during the stripping, in which case it would be better for individual voices to read the psalms (perhaps from the back of the church) than for them to be said antiphonally or responsorially. A choir or cantors may keep their hand-held candles lit until the end of the psalmody, after which silence is kept and the church is left in semi-darkness, with sufficient light for members of the congregation to go to and from the Altar of Repose.

## The Watch

The Watch of the Passion continues until midnight. It is common for a list to have been placed in church for individuals to sign up to watch at a particular time, to ensure that there is no period when no one is present. Individual communities will also need to consider issues relating to personal safety if one or two people are to be left in church on their own.

TS suggests passages from the Gospel of John and psalms which may be used at regular intervals during the Watch (p. 304). Alternatively, the Watch may take place in silence. Just before midnight the Gospel of the Watch may be read, followed by the Collect of Good Friday, and the people may depart in silence. All candles on the Altar of Repose should be extinguished except for one white lamp which should remain lit throughout the night.

If possible, before the church is opened on Good Friday, flowers and candles should be removed from the Altar of Repose so that, as Elliott describes it, a 'simpler form of adoration' may continue up to the Liturgy of Good Friday. The single white lamp should remain lit while the sacrament remains there.

## Good Friday

While we concentrate mostly on present practical concerns in this book, in the case of Good Friday it is especially important to be aware of the history of the liturgy of the day since it has a particularly important bearing on how the rite is to be celebrated today in terms of the difference between past and present assumptions and attitudes. Historically speaking, the earliest parts of the Liturgy of Good Friday are the solemn chanting of the passion according to John and the veneration of the cross, originally a relic of the cross. Both occurred in Jerusalem in the fourth century. The liturgy has undergone expansion and enrichment, but these elements remain at its heart. The papal liturgy introduced solemn prayers, eventually nine in number. In Roman parishes, in addition to the passion reading and the veneration, Communion was received from the sacrament reserved the previous evening. However, along with these practical elements, the mood became increasingly sombre in the Middle Ages, and as the TS introduction to the Passiontide resources reminds us, anti-Semitic overtones entered the texts (TS: p. 259). For these and other reasons, the cross and its veneration became the focus of the rite, accompanied by the singing of the Reproaches (*Improperia*), openly blaming the Jews for the crucifixion. Twentieth-century reforms removed most of the anti-Semitic material, although some would argue that the singing of the Reproaches, even with the modified text provided, still implies the opprobrium of former times. This blending of especially ancient liturgical forms with the social and religious controversies of the past means exercising the greatest of care when planning and celebrating this liturgy, as TS makes clear:

This places a double responsibility on those who lead the keeping of Holy Week today: to be faithful to the act of collective memory, but also to be sensitive to the ways in which an unreflecting use of traditional texts (like the Reproaches) can perpetuate a strain of Christian anti-Semitism.

(TS: p. 259)

In practical terms, the emphasis ought to be on simplicity if the focus on the passion narrative and the cross rather than elaborate ceremonial is to be clear. These central elements are contained within a fivefold structure that is still relatively simple, as set out by TS (p. 305): Gathering, Liturgy of the Word, Proclamation of the Cross, Prayers of Intercession, Liturgy of the Sacrament. Within these sections there is nevertheless room for variation, as will be discussed below.

Visually the church should be as it was left after the liturgy of Maundy Thursday evening – stripped of textile hangings and moveable liturgical furnishings such as candlesticks so as to leave a starkly empty space. This impression is vital to the celebration of the Good Friday liturgy, partly in that those entering the church for the liturgy are rightly taken aback by it in the daylight, even if they were present in the darkness of the previous evening. In this way the attention is drawn to the central actions as they unfold. The other essential characteristic that must be present right from the beginning is silence, a concern which should also affect the musical provision:

Silence is a significant part of the observance of Good Friday, and silence at the points indicated is integral to the service. It is appropriate for the organ to be used only to accompany singing.

(TS: p. 306)

Morning Prayer on Good Friday should be celebrated in the stripped space resulting from the Maundy Thursday liturgy the evening before.

The Liturgy of Good Friday may be celebrated at a number of possible times of day. It may stand alone in the middle of the day, or in the evening. Alternatively it may be part of a 'Three Hours' service, typically beginning at noon and concluding at 3 p.m., for which various patterns are possible, including for example:

- The Litany in Procession.
- The Preaching of the Passion.
- The Liturgy of Good Friday.

Local imagination and custom are encouraged here to find a pastorally appropriate pattern. While the Liturgy may be celebrated at other times of the day according to local custom, the clear emphasis it receives in TS underlines its paramount importance – it should be the principal service of the day. The primacy of the Liturgy does not prevent other services taking place on Good Friday – the Daily Offices, and in many places an ecumenical act of witness in town centres or perhaps an evening celebration of 'Unity at the Cross'. There should be no celebration of the Eucharist on Good Friday.

The president should be vested as for the Eucharist in a red chasuble. Other ordained ministers wear albs and red stoles or a red High Mass set (chasuble, dalmatic and tunicle) and servers plain albs, surplices or cottas. Incense is not used. There should not be a crucifer so as not to detract from the liturgical cross at the centre of the liturgical drama. At the time of its entry this cross may be accompanied by acolytes and their lights, who also carry them when and if the blessed sacrament is brought in, but not at the beginning and end of the Liturgy. For Holy Communion using elements consecrated at the Maundy Liturgy, there need to be made ready a fair linen altar cloth, corporal, lavabo bowl and towel. If the sacrament is to be brought in solemnly from the place of repose, a red humeral veil may also be provided at the Altar of Repose.

## The Gathering

If another act of worship has preceded the Liturgy, there should be a distinct space between the end of the former and the beginning of the latter. In any case the ministers and servers will need to prepare for the Liturgy. If the Liturgy alone is being celebrated, the congregation should assemble in silence, and there should be no music played or sung here or at the entry of the ministers.

Entering in silence, the ministers approach the altar. The president and other ministers either kneel or prostrate themselves on the pavement or other flooring of the sanctuary for a time of silent prayer, during which the servers and people kneel. The prostration is done in this way:

- Enter.
- Bow.
- Kneel.
- Prostrate with arms outstretched forwards.
- Remain prostrate for a period of silence.
- Rise to kneeling position (taking time from the president).
- Stand.

Those prostrating must take care. It would be a good idea if very fragile vestments were not used on this occasion if the ministers are to prostrate themselves. All rise with the president, who goes to the chair, and the other ministers and servers to their places with dignity. All remain standing. The first spoken words are those of the collect, for which the two CW options are given (TS: p. 307). The president does not say 'Let us pray', but with hands in the *orans* position begins the collect directly. After the collect, all sit.

## The Liturgy of the Word

The Old and New Testament readings which follow are specified in TS (p. 308): Isaiah 52.13—end of 53 and Hebrews 10.16–25 or 4.14–16; 5.7–9. On this occasion others should not be substituted. A period of silence after each reading is especially important on this day. Between the readings Psalm 22 is sung or said either in part or complete. A suitable hymn (not over-long, perhaps 'Glory be to Jesus') or canticle is sung after the second reading.

Unlike the Passion reading on Palm Sunday which varies over the three-year cycle, the Passion reading on Good Friday should be that according to John 18.1—19.42 or a sensible abbreviation if felt absolutely necessary – the power lies in the unfolding drama. As with the Palm Sunday Passion, this is an opportunity for creativity and imagination in terms of how the Passion is read and by whom, and the same possibilities hold good (see Palm Sunday above and CW *Proclaiming the Passion*). However, in planning the liturgy of Holy Week and Easter, consideration might be given to employing a different method of reading the Passion on Good Friday from that used on Palm Sunday. Two enacted versions are likely to involve considerable numbers in a lot of preparation – in some communities this may be possible. But there is a case for using a simpler method on Good Friday in keeping with the starkness of the day, and in contrast to the richness of John's account. This may therefore be the occasion for a single reader (who should be an accomplished reader if the text is to be most effective) or the traditional three cantors and the choir. Again, all normally stand throughout the reading, standing as the cantors or readers enter. At the words 'he gave up his spirit', all genuflect or kneel and rise with the president. The special introduction and conclusion without congregational response are used, and there are no lights or incense. Verses from a suitable Bach Passion Chorale might be sung at intervals during the Passion. The Passion should be followed by a period of silence (perhaps one minute) during which all remain in the places from which they read or sung. Then readers or cantors return to their seats, the preacher moving to the pulpit or legilium as they do so. A sermon should be preached at the Liturgy.

## The Proclamation of the Cross

In TS the Proclamation of the Cross may occur either here or following the Prayers of Intercession (rubric, TS: p. 309). The rubrics occupying less than half a page in TS, precisely how this is done depends very much on local custom, the nature of the liturgical space and the availability of musical resources. In some places the outer vestments are removed (but not the stoles) by the ministers wearing them before the cross is brought in, or immediately before the veneration (see Elliott 2002: pp. 119–20).

Interpreting the rubrics in TS (p. 309) in turn:

'*A wooden cross is brought into the church and placed in the sight of the people.*'

The deacon (preferably) or the president goes with the acolytes to the place from which the cross is to be collected, at which the acolytes' candles should also be ready and lit. The minister picks up the cross, holding it aloft in front of the body, the figure of Christ facing the people, and enters with it preceded by the acolytes. The exact size and style of the cross may vary considerably in practice. It may be a plain cross or a crucifix, meaning an image of the crucified Christ, not of Christ reigning from the cross. It should be of a size which makes it a considerable visual symbol and appropriate focus of the devotion of the people, while being sufficiently portable.

*'As the cross is carried in, the procession may stop three times and one of the following versicles and responses may be said or sung.'*

This rubric invites the use of the traditional rite of the entry of the cross. The cross may already be veiled with a purple cloth when it enters, and gradually unveiled at each of the three stations. Alternatively it may be unveiled throughout. It makes dramatic sense for the cross to be brought in from the liturgical west end of the church, all turning to face it as it moves through the building. The first station is made near the rear of the nave, the acolytes turning to face the cross. Its entry is acclaimed using one of the two texts, both versions of the traditional form, preferably intoned by the deacon, and rising in pitch at each station. The second station might be halfway up the nave, and the final one on the chancel or sanctuary step, the minister now turning to face the people with the cross and intoning the versicle for the third and final time. At each station, all genuflect (including the congregation) as the cross is acclaimed.

Alternatively, the cross could simply be brought in during the singing of a hymn, perhaps 'When I survey the wondrous cross', and placed in a stand at the chancel step.

*'Appropriate devotions may follow, which may include any or all of the following or other suitable anthems. Traditionally the hymn "Faithful Cross" ("Crux Fidelis") is also sung.'*

'Appropriate devotions' can be taken to include the actual physical reverencing of the cross by an embrace or a kiss where this is the custom. It is perfectly possible, however, to position the cross in such a way as to allow a variety of responses according to the devotional wishes of individuals, for example at the entrance to the sanctuary so that people may simply kneel at the altar rail if they so desire. Indeed, the modern Roman rite says that 'the faithful may, where necessary, venerate the cross in silence, without leaving their places'

(SM: p. 272). If the traditional reverencing is to take place, at least by some, the two acolytes put down their candles either side of the cross, and take it from the minister. The minister and other ministers now venerate the cross. They may do so by making a solemn approach, processing slowly down a side aisle and up the centre aisle, keeping a distance between them, the president leading. In some places this may be done barefoot, in which case they need to pause in the side aisle to remove their footwear (members of the congregation may also reverence the cross barefoot if they wish). The president genuflects on approaching the cross, kneels before it and kisses the feet of the image of the crucified Christ, rises, genuflects again and moves on. The other ministers follow, then those of the people who wish to do so, genuflecting as they approach and again when they have venerated the cross. The acolytes wait until all have venerated, at which point the cross is held for them by a sacristan or other servers so that they may approach and do so themselves. While the cross is being venerated by the congregation, the president and other ministers return to their places and sit.

The devotions used during the veneration may indeed include the *Crux fidelis* (e.g. NEH 517). TS also provides two versions of the Reproaches as Anthem 1, Version 1 and Version 2 (TS: pp. 310–14). The first, most similar to the traditional text and interspersed with the *Trisagion*, and the second, alternative text, both take note of the associated sensitivities referred to above. Anthems 2, 3 and 4 (pp. 314–15) are much shorter texts which may be used in any combination in addition to or instead of Anthem 1. Other hymns and anthems may be sung, of which there are many possibilities, but all should be conducive to the veneration proceeding in the midst of all. The Acclamations (TS: p. 315) which may conclude the veneration are responsorial in form and traditional and, as with all else, are most effective when sung.

When the cross has been thus venerated and acclaimed, it is taken to its place in the sanctuary where it will remain visible. This should, if possible, be on or near the altar itself, for which a suitable stand will need to be provided. The cross should be carried to the sanctuary by the deacon or president, accompanied by the acolytes, who collect their lights as the minister takes the cross from the person who has been holding it for them. Processing with dignity to the sanctuary, the minister places the cross in its stand, and genuflects.

The acolytes place their candles either side of the altar (or even upon it either side of the cross if they have suitable bases).

## The Prayers of Intercession

The Prayers of Intercession, the 'Solemn Prayers' of the traditional liturgy, now follow (TS: pp. 316–18), introduced by the president in the words provided. They may be sung to a tone by the deacon, who sings the biddings, the president singing the collect. The deacon may stand at the legilium, the president at the chair. Alternative prayers may be used, but the use of the default text is strongly recommended for its comprehensiveness and suitability. Each section comprises a bidding, silence, response and collect. The language is rich, and many of the collects of ancient provenance, including the fine prayer which begins 'O God of unchangeable power and eternal light', the original context of which was the Paschal Vigil, as in the Gelasian Sacramentary.

If there is to be no Liturgy of the Sacrament, the Lord's Prayer follows the Prayers of Intercession, and the liturgy moves directly to the conclusion (TS: p. 320).

## The Liturgy of the Sacrament

Many communities will, however, celebrate the Liturgy of the Sacrament after the Prayers of Intercession, if the sacrament was taken to an Altar of Repose at the Maundy Thursday liturgy. TS does *not* envisage a full celebration of the Eucharist, a practice found in some places but without historical precedent and in danger of drawing attention away from the cross.

After the Prayers of Intercession, a server puts the altar cloth, corporal and book on the altar. Meanwhile the acolytes and the deacon (preferably) or the president go in formal procession to the Altar of Repose. They genuflect, and while the minister kneels, one of the acolytes places the humeral veil (if used) on the shoulders of the minister, assisting with the clasp at the front as necessary. Then the acolytes pick up a second set of lights which have been prepared and lit beside the Altar of Repose. The minister rises, goes to the altar (opens the tabernacle), genuflects, and in the folds of the humeral veil picks up the ciborium containing the consecrated bread. If Holy

Communion is to be given in both kinds, another minister collects the vessel of wine. However, it is entirely appropriate to give Communion in one kind on this occasion, with appropriate prior teaching on the matter, although TS assumes both elements (TS: p. 319). Even if it is used here, the practice of administering Communion in one kind should *never* occur at a celebration of the Eucharist, since receiving in both kinds is the normative practice of the Church of England.

The people stand as the procession returns to the sanctuary, and the minister places the ciborium on the corporal and genuflects. For ease of visibility this may be done from the liturgical western side of the altar, facing east. If a humeral veil has been used it is now removed by a server. The acolytes place their candles in suitable places either side of the altar or, if there is room and their bases suitable, upon the altar next to the pair already there either side of the cross. The president either remains facing east, or goes to the other side of the altar to face west, and introduces the Lord's Prayer. The president invites the people to Communion in one of the forms given (TS: p. 319). Holy Communion is then given in one or both kinds, either in silence or during a hymn or anthem. Any consecrated elements remaining should be consumed. The president's fingers are washed in a lavabo bowl, the corporal is folded and removed.

At this point the liturgy may conclude simply with the post-Communion (TS: p. 320), to which a Prayer over the People may be added, for example:

*President*   Lord,
send down your abundant blessing
upon your people who have devoutly recalled the death
  of your Son
in the sure hope of the resurrection.
Grant them pardon; bring them comfort.
May their faith grow stronger
and their eternal salvation be assured.
We ask this through Christ our Lord.

(SM: p. 277)

In TS the first optional post-Communion (p. 320) is the Memorial of the Cross which, as Eric Milner-White says in the introduction to his *Procession of Passion Prayers*, 'intertwined itself with the Office of our Lady' in the day hours (Milner-White 1956: p. xiii). One of the prayers should be used with or without a further Prayer over the People as above. These prayers also conclude the service if there has been no Liturgy of the Sacrament. No blessing or dismissal is given, and ministers and people depart in silence. It is customary to genuflect to the cross while it is on the altar (ministers and people alike). The people may depart informally (but silently) in all directions.

An alternative conclusion is suggested (TS: p. 320) which involves the reading of the Gospel of the Burial of Christ (John 19.38–42) and the carrying out of the cross. If this is used, the earlier Passion reading should end at John 19.37. The adoption of this conclusion would, however, remove the cross from the altar and thus from the sight of those who wish to pray before it after the Liturgy and during the rest of the day. It is appropriate for the cross and the burning candles either side to remain on the altar as a focus until after the final service of the day, which may be Evening Prayer, Night Prayer, or an ecumenical Evening Service, for example, but depending on when the Liturgy has been celebrated. If there is to be a performance of a devotional work in the evening, if the cross is still visible it could remain.

# Holy Saturday

By tradition, Holy Saturday (which should *never* be called 'Easter Saturday') is a day starkly devoid of any complex liturgical celebration. The Offices are said (see ALG 5: p. 98), and should themselves be in simpler form, but there is no celebration of the Eucharist and no Liturgy of the Day. The church is in the bare state it has been in since the night of Maundy Thursday. The silence which fell then should be maintained liturgically on Holy Saturday as far as is sensibly and practically possible.

However, it is by practical necessity a day of preparation. It is an opportunity to extensively clean the church, revitalizing the liturgical space for the most solemn liturgy of the year. In this sense it is vital to the liturgy, and part of the observance of the Triduum. If members of the community are encouraged to come along and help to clean and prepare for Easter, it offers a unique opportunity for fellowship which, given the nature of the day, is almost 'liturgical' in its significance – the work of the people, an offering of souls and bodies to enable *the* Liturgy of liturgies to take place with as much joy and commitment as possible.

In the afternoon and evening, preparations for the Easter Vigil will almost certainly need to begin. If there is to be a celebration of Evening Prayer, it is preferable that not too much of 'Easter' has been put in place. It is also important that Evening Prayer is entirely that of Easter Eve, not in any sense an anticipation of Easter itself, as the introduction to the Easter Liturgy in TS makes clear (TS: p. 323).

# 3

# The Easter Liturgy

Rejoice, heavenly powers! Sing, choirs of angels!
O universe, dance around God's throne!
Jesus Christ, our King, is risen!
Sound the victorious trumpet of salvation!

This is the night when Jesus Christ vanquished hell,
broke the chains of death
and rose triumphant from the grave.

(The Exsultet, TS: pp. 410–11)

## Planning the Easter Liturgy

'This is the night.' The great Paschal Vigil, celebrated between dusk on Holy Saturday and dawn on Easter Day, is the Christian liturgy *par excellence*. Joyful and confident in its dramatic proclamation of the resurrection of Jesus Christ, it is the most important celebration in the liturgical calendar and the high point of the Christian year. Light, water, bread and wine – sacramental elements which have been gradually and deliberately removed from the worshipping space during the celebration of the Triduum – are restored to the Christian community during the Easter Liturgy, renewed by the transforming power of Christ's resurrection.

TS devotes more than 100 pages to the Easter Liturgy, providing resources not only for two forms of the Paschal Vigil (which it refers to as the Easter Liturgy), but also for other liturgical celebrations on Easter Day. As with the other traditional Holy Week liturgies, the celebration of the Paschal Vigil was, until relatively recently, the exclusive preserve of those within the Catholic tradition. With its rich range of resources, TS sets out to encourage members of the Church of England from a variety of traditions to make creative use of some of the ancient symbolic acts with which Christians have celebrated the resurrection of Christ. The guidance which follows can very profitably be read in conjunction with the sections in ALG 4 concerned with the symbols of water and light, particularly where they deal with the Easter Liturgy (ALG 4: pp. 31–3, 68–72).

Each community is faced with a number of issues which need to be addressed before more detailed decisions are made about how the Easter Liturgy is celebrated. Although liturgists may be confident in asserting that the Easter Liturgy, with its four principal elements of Service of Light, Vigil of Readings, Liturgy of Initiation and Liturgy of the Eucharist (TS: pp. 326–7), is the most important service of the year, that is not how it is perceived in many parishes, and it may, in fact, attract a much smaller congregation than the weekly Sunday morning Eucharist. If the Church is to have confidence in the celebration of the Easter Liturgy, not least as a means of formation of the Christian community and a tool for mission, then clergy and lay leaders must take responsibility for teaching about its significance. For those approaching this material for the first time, one option might be to incorporate some of the material from the Service of Light into the main act of worship on Easter Day (TS: pp. 401–7), but this is a liturgy whose essential symbolism, that of the triumph of light over darkness, depends on it being celebrated at night or before dawn.

If it is to begin in darkness, a further decision needs to be made about whether it should begin after dark (often from 8 p.m. onwards) or in the early hours of the morning (around 5 a.m.). Giles is very critical of an evening celebration. 'This will never do . . . the rite at this hour sends you home in the dark . . . You are left with an anti-climactic sense that, after all the fuss, Easter is yet to come' (Giles 2008: pp. 137–8). In an ideal liturgical world, an early-morning Vigil with the celebration of the Eucharist at dawn followed by a celebratory breakfast is undoubtedly the ideal and has become well established in a number of communities. In others, however, pastoral reasons may suggest otherwise, and it must therefore be left up to individual churches to decide what timing makes the Paschal Vigil the centre point of their liturgical life. One consideration is likely to be whether there are candidates for baptism and/or confirmation and, if so, what time will best suit them and their supporters. Whatever time is chosen, the liturgy must not begin before it is dark.

Another issue which needs to be addressed is the relationship between the Paschal Vigil and any other liturgies which are celebrated on Easter Day. In many communities, even if the majority wish to make the Paschal Vigil *the* celebration of Easter, this will be a gradual process which is likely to take several years, and not a transition that is going to be made in the space of one Holy Week. It is still customary in many places for the main service on Easter morning (and, in some places, an early-morning Eucharist) to attract a number of worshippers, some of them communicants, who are not regular members of the Sunday congregation. For them that service will be *their* celebration of Easter. Therefore, while working towards raising the profile of the Paschal Vigil in the spiritual lives of regular worshipping members of the community, the significance and importance of other Easter services should not be underestimated, including those which may be attended by significant numbers of children. Some excellent all-age material for Easter can be found in the second volume of *Together for a Season* (Ambrose 2007: pp. 122–53).

The relationship between the Paschal Vigil and other liturgical celebrations also has a bearing on which elements of the Easter Liturgy are included as part of the 'Vigil'. It has become customary in some places to divide the Easter Liturgy by celebrating the Service of Light, Vigil of Readings and Liturgy of Initiation after dark on Holy Saturday and postponing the Eucharist until the following morning. TS cites this as a possibility, along with postponing both Initiation and Eucharist until Easter Day, or celebrating the Vigil of Readings on its own at night or in the early morning or, indeed, omitting it altogether (TS: p. 327). While pastoral reasons may be thought to justify such a division (for example, in cathedrals, to allow the bishop to celebrate Christian initiation within the context of the Paschal Vigil, and the candidates to make their first Communion in their home parishes later on Easter Day), there is a more important theological and liturgical consideration relating to the unity of the whole liturgy which is of greater importance than the issue of timing referred to above. TS alludes to this when it says:

> However the Easter celebrations are structured and conducted, all possible variations derive from the one Easter Liturgy, which needs to be seen as a whole even if it is celebrated in distinct stages.

> (TS: p. 327)

Although this goes some way to addressing the issue of the integrity of the whole, it is not so much that the four elements need to be celebrated together for the sake of the liturgy from which they are derived, as that they need to be experienced as a whole and as part of one celebration, for the sake of those who participate in this concluding act in the drama of salvation. Those who gather in darkness to celebrate the presence of the risen Christ in the kindling of a new fire, in the proclamation of God's mighty acts and in the lives of those who are born again in the waters of the font, also need to recognize and receive him in the breaking of the bread. Whether the Vigil of Readings or Service of Light comes first, the Easter Liturgy has a theological logic and coherence, with one element naturally leading to the next. To destroy this spiritual momentum by dividing the liturgy is to injure the integrity of the rite and compromise its transforming power.

A final consideration has already been alluded to and relates to the order in which the first two elements of the rite are celebrated. TS provides two complete forms of the Easter Liturgy together with some useful historical background for each (pp. 324–5). Pattern A begins with the Service of Light which is followed by the Vigil of Readings. In this order 'the history of our salvation in the Scriptures is heard in the light of the Easter mystery' (p. 324). Pattern B has the readings first and then the Service of Light; thus 'a sense of expectation gradually increases until the service reaches its climax in the revelation of the resurrection' (p. 324).

There is much to commend either pattern and TS provides some helpful advice to assist communities in deciding which would be most appropriate for them. Although it would be possible to alternate between them, using Pattern A one year and Pattern B the next, there is something to be said for deciding on one pattern and sticking to it so as to provide a degree of continuity and familiarity at a time of year when everything is quite deliberately different from the norm. TS also offers a third, more flexible pattern which suggests how Vigil material might be used at a Dawn Service, perhaps in a field, on a hilltop, by a river or on a beach (pp. 325, 398–400). For the purposes of this guide, Pattern A will be followed, with reference to Pattern B as and when necessary.

Having decided when the Easter Liturgy should be celebrated, how it will relate to other Easter services and what elements it will contain, there are at least two further points to consider. First, more than any other service during Holy Week, the Easter Liturgy lends itself to the creative use of space. It has already been suggested that it may be possible for the congregation to gather outside the church for the blessing of the new fire and lighting of the Easter Candle, to sit in the nave for the Vigil of Readings, move to the font for the Liturgy of Initiation and then process to the sanctuary for the Liturgy of the Sacrament (pp. 85, 88). Any such decisions obviously depend on the space available and the number of people attending. The Easter Liturgy is rarely a short service, and so, wherever possible, movement is to be encouraged. TS suggests that, if Pattern B is followed, it is particularly appropriate to have the Vigil of Readings in a separate building, such as a church hall, or even outside. Equally, if several parishes are combining to celebrate the Easter Liturgy, it may be possible to process from one to the other, if distances allow. There is also scope for ecumenical co-operation in this service, and dividing the liturgy between two different church buildings, even if it means going to separate altars for the Liturgy of the Eucharist.

A second point, which affects the use of space, relates to the Liturgy of Initiation and whether any candidates are to be baptized and/or confirmed during the Paschal Vigil. Although liturgical scholars are no longer convinced that Easter was the one time in the year when, in the early centuries of the Church's life, Christian Initiation was celebrated, this does not alter the fact that the Church's celebration of Christ's passover from death to life is an entirely appropriate time for those who have turned to Christ to become members of his body by being baptized into his death and resurrection (Romans 6.3–4), particularly if they have been preparing for this during Lent. If confirmation is also celebrated, the bishop should preside over the whole rite. The *Ceremonial of Bishops* provides detailed notes on episcopal presidency at the Paschal Vigil which can easily be adapted to the CW rite (*Ceremonial of Bishops* 1989: pp. 113–21).

## Preparations for the Easter Liturgy

As with many of the Holy Week liturgies, a number of preparations are required for the Paschal Vigil. Gold or white is the liturgical colour and, if churches have them, altar frontals and hangings need to be put in place before the liturgy begins. (The custom of beginning the Vigil in purple and changing to white after the Liturgy of Initiation (Fortescue and O'Connell 1948: p. 307) is no longer practised.) In addition to flower arrangements, appropriate banners and other decorations may be displayed. These can have ribbons attached to them, and ribbon may also be tied round the processional cross at the point at which the base of the cross and the pole meet. If the church possesses a processional cross and a processional crucifix, the former is more appropriate during Eastertide, and should be placed in its stand in the sanctuary, as it will not be carried in the entrance procession. Acolyte candles should also be in their stocks and the Book of the Gospels placed on the altar.

In many churches an Easter Garden is prepared on Holy Saturday. This may take a number of forms, but will usually include a model of Christ's tomb (with a stone which can be rolled away, revealing the grave-clothes) and, in another part of the scene, the three crosses of Calvary, with a white cloth draped over the arms of the one in the centre. The garden will often contain a variety of plants and shrubs and may be blessed on Easter morning (p. 85) and used as a focus for devotion throughout the Easter season (p. 88).

A fire needs to be prepared in a suitable place, preferably outside. If possible, the fire should be large enough so that it can be lit as the first people arrive, and act as a focal point as they gather (although Irvine warns against a large fire becoming a 'spectacle in itself'; ALG 4: p. 70). At least one person should be given responsibility for looking after the fire, not only during the Service of Light, but also once the procession has entered the church. If an outdoor fire is not possible, a small brazier may be set up in the church porch or another suitable place but, as Elliott notes, 'every effort should be made to avoid using a portable barbeque' (Elliott 2002: p. 134)!

The Easter Candle should be of a size appropriate to the liturgical space. Marked with a cross, the Greek letters Alpha (A) and Omega ($\Omega$) and the four numerals of the current year (TS: p. 408), this is the principal symbolic focus for the presence of the risen Christ, and its size and design should reflect that, as should the candlestick in which it is placed. Decorated with flowers and ribbons, the candlestick's position will depend on the layout of the building. TS suggests that it should stand in the 'midst of the building' (p. 335). Although such a position emphasizes its importance, if Pattern A is followed, it is particularly important that it should be placed near to the ambo, lectern or pulpit from where the scriptures will be read. A stylus (a pointed, metallic pen-shaped object) to mark the candle, the five incense studs (TS also permits the use of nails; p. 335) and a taper or splinter of wood should be put on a small tray so that they can be conveniently passed to the president during the Service of Light. As this will take place in the dark, it is helpful if the places where the incense studs will be inserted can be marked on the candle before the service, so that the studs can be easily inserted when the time comes. If incense is to be used for the Liturgy, charcoal should be placed near the fire so that it can be lit from it, together with a pair of tongs.

If a number of congregations join together to celebrate the Easter Liturgy, only one Easter Candle should be used. TS suggests that, 'if it is desired to take Easter Candles back to other churches, they may be lit from the first candle at the end of the service and carried in procession out of the building' (p. 331, note 7). It also provides a rite for Welcoming the Easter Candle into the Church (p. 418), which may be used when a church's Easter Candle has been lit at an Easter Liturgy celebrated elsewhere.

Those attending the Paschal Vigil should be asked to bring bells and anything else that they may wish to ring, blow or hit to create a joyful noise at beginning of the *Gloria in Excelsis*. Bells should also be put out for the ministers and, if people are willing to clear up the mess they make, party-poppers can also be distributed around the church! Sparklers are also popular in some places but, if they are used, careful thought needs to be given to how they can be used and disposed of safely.

If the rites of Christian Initiation are to be celebrated, the usual preparations need to be made. If possible, the water should be carried to the font in a ewer by a candidate or sponsor at the appropriate point in the liturgy. If there are no candidates for baptism or confirmation, a member of the congregation can carry the water. An empty holy water bucket should be placed near the font with an aspergilium or, preferably, a large sprig of rosemary.

Holy water stoups should still be empty, as should the tabernacle or aumbry, with the door open. A lamp should be placed beside the place of reservation, ready to be lit as soon as the sacrament is restored. If there are any statues or other images in the church, lamps should be prepared beside them, so that they can be lit during the *Gloria*, along with the candles on the principal altar and on any other altars in the church. No candles should be lit before the service.

The president wears a gold or white chasuble throughout the Easter Liturgy. If other priests are present, it is appropriate for them to concelebrate, especially if the Eucharist of the Last Supper was concelebrated. If there is a deacon, he or she has an important and distinctive liturgical ministry in this rite. If there is no deacon a concelebrant or assistant priest may carry out the diaconal roles or, lacking anyone else, they may be performed by the president. If required, a lay minister may carry the Easter Candle and, if none of the clergy is confident to sing the Exsultet, it may be sung by a cantor, omitting the *sursum corda*. Wherever possible, the Exsultet should be sung.

## The Service of Light

If Pattern A is used the congregation should, weather permitting, gather outside the church around the fire (TS: p. 331, note 3). If it is wet then people go straight to the church, where the lights should be dimmed and no organ music played. If there is sufficient space, it is better for them to gather around the place where the fire will be lit rather than going to sit in their places. Wherever the Service of Light takes place, hand-held candles are distributed to everyone (except for candidates for baptism, who will receive theirs at the end of the liturgy) as well as orders of service. The Paschal Vigil is an occasion when the service booklet should helpfully contain everything that is needed for the service, including the hymns.

The ministers process informally to join the congregation at the fire, led by the thurifer carrying the empty thurible. If there is a choir, they can gather with the people rather than processing with the ministers. Since the Easter Candle is the principal symbolic focus of the risen Christ, the processional cross and acolyte candles are not carried. The deacon carries the Easter Candle. If there are sufficient servers, one carries the book containing the president's texts and another a torch, in case it is too dark to read them. Other servers carry hand-held candles.

When all have gathered around the fire, the Service of Light begins. Although TS does not print the Trinitarian invocation and presidential greeting with which CW Order One begins, there is no reason why these should not be used. The president then introduces the rite and blesses the fire (TS: p. 334). Two prayers are provided. Neither explicitly asks God to bless the fire. However, the first text may be adapted as follows:

*President*    Let us pray.
           Eternal God,
           who made this most holy night
           to shine with the brightness of your one true light:
           + *make this new fire holy, inflame us with your love,*
           and bring us to the radiance of your heavenly glory;
           through Jesus Christ our Lord.

In the modern rite the president sings or says the prayer of blessing with hands joined and makes the sign of the cross where indicated. The censing of the fire is no longer required, nor need it be sprinkled with holy water (Fortescue and O'Connell 1948: p. 310).

As soon as the fire has been blessed, a thurifer takes a light from it and uses it to ignite the charcoal, which is placed in the thurible. While this is happening the president marks the Easter Candle. The two diagrams which explain how this should be done also include the words which accompany each action (TS: pp. 408–9).

The president then lights the Easter Candle from the fire while saying the prescribed formula (TS: p. 335). As Giles notes, this is sometimes easier said than done (Giles 2008: p. 142), and a splinter of wood can often be used to transfer the flame from the fire to the candle more easily than a taper. In windy weather it is quite possible that the candle will go out before it reaches the church. If this happens it can be relit by a server with a lighter or matches.

Once the candle is lit, the president puts incense into the thurible, and the deacon, carrying the Easter Candle, moves to the entrance to the church and sings 'The Light of Christ', to which all respond **'Thanks be to God'**. The thurifer leads the procession into the darkened church, followed by the deacon carrying the candle, the president, the MC (if there is one), other ministers and servers, and the choir and congregation. The acclamation 'The Light of Christ' is made three times, each time beginning on a higher note. Giles suggests that the congregation's candles should be lit from the Easter Candle 'as soon as it is blessed' (Giles 2008: p. 142). The more traditional practice of a gradual lighting of the hand-held candles may be preferred (Fortescue and O'Connell 1948: pp. 312–13), not least since it allows the light to spread more slowly and the procession to move more smoothly. After the first acclamation only the president's candle is lit. At the second station, which is made in the middle of the church, the light is passed back so that the candles of any other clergy and the servers can be lit (the modern Roman rite directs that everyone's candles should be lit at this point: Elliott 2002: p. 278). At the final station, which may be at the entrance to the sanctuary or in another prominent place, everyone's candles are lit, either by the servers or by encouraging the congregation to approach the Easter Candle and light their candles directly from it before moving to their places.

Once the people's candles have been lit the Easter Candle is put in its stand. The ceremonial associated with the preparation for the Exsultet, the great Easter Proclamation, is similar to that at the Gospel. The president puts on incense at the chair. The deacon approaches to ask for a blessing, and the president responds with these words:

| | |
|---|---|
| *President* | The Lord be in your heart and on your lips, that you may worthily proclaim his Easter praise. In the name of the Father, and of the Son, + and of the Holy Spirit. |
| *Deacon* | Amen. |

In the Roman rite the blessing is omitted if the Exsultet is sung by one who is not a deacon (*The Sacramentary* 1985: p. 174) Having been blessed, the deacon moves to the Easter Candle which, if possible, should stand next to the ambo, lectern or pulpit from which the readings will be proclaimed. The deacon first censes the book containing the text of the Exsultet with three double swings, and then walks around the candle censing it. If the Exsultet is to be sung from the pulpit, it would make sense to cense the candle first and then the book. The ministers and people remain standing, holding their candles, as the Exsultet is sung. Various forms are provided in TS. The RSCM has published a version of the main text (TS: pp. 336–7), with optional responses, set to the traditional Roman tone. Alternatively, the main text of the Exsultet may be sung to the tone, and the introduction to the metrical version, 'Sing, choirs of heaven', to a tune such as 'Woodlands'. In an appendix, TS also provides an alternative ending to the main text, which refers to the flame being 'fed by melting wax conceived by mother bee', an image popularized in the Franco–Roman Church (TS: p. 412). There is also a much shorter responsorial form (p. 413) as well as a ten-verse metrical version, from which verses may be sung by different groups of people and/or individuals, as well as by everyone (pp. 414–15). In all versions references to 'night' may be replaced by 'day' if sung after daybreak.

## The Vigil

At the end of the Exsultet TS suggests that a hymn may be sung 'during which lights are taken from the Easter Candle to illuminate the Bible from which the Vigil readings will be read' (p. 338). Although candles either side of the ambo should be lit, a hymn at this point in the liturgy is unnecessary and likely to interrupt the movement from the Service of Light to the Vigil. TS provides a form of words with which the president may introduce the Vigil readings. It is also possible for the president to replace this with a more informal and, perhaps, fuller introduction. If this is done, care should be taken so that what is said here is not repeated in the sermon which will follow later.

If Pattern B is followed, the Easter Liturgy begins with the Vigil of Readings. As already mentioned, TS suggests that it should 'be kept in a place other than the church' and that a source of light, possibly a fire, oil lamp or electric light, should be provided to enable the Scriptures to be read (p. 351). TS ritualizes the lighting of this light by prefacing it with a reading from Genesis 1.1 (if this is not to be read during the Vigil) and following it with one of two prayers (p. 354). Recognizing that there is a danger that this light could be confused with the Easter light (TS: p. 324), to give the provision of a light which is purely functional a place within the liturgy seems unnecessary. It would be better, perhaps, to begin Pattern B with the president's words of introduction (TS: p. 354).

TS provides no fewer than 22 Old Testament passages from which the Vigil readings may be taken (pp. 375–97), of which it is considered 'desirable' that Genesis 1 should be read, and the reading from Exodus 14, the crossing of the Red Sea, always be used. The number of readings chosen will depend on several factors, not least the timing of the service and whether baptism and/or confirmation is to be celebrated within the Easter Liturgy. The Roman rite provides seven Old Testament readings and requires that at least three, or in 'special cases' two, must be read. The number of readings should not be reduced just because the Vigil is considered to be the least interesting element of an otherwise dramatic liturgy.

In addition to Genesis 1 and Exodus 14 the choice of the other readings may vary from year to year. TS gives some helpful guidance and suggests five themes (pp. 373–4) which may be used. It is particularly important at this service that the readings are read clearly, and there is a lot to be said for rehearsing readers beforehand. Where a number of readings are used, care should be taken to involve readers of different ages, men, women and children, representing different areas of the community's life. A psalm or canticle follows each reading. If possible they should be sung, and they may take various forms. (It may be desirable for the person who reads the account of the Exodus to be the cantor for the canticle which follows.) If musical resources permit, modern responsorial and metrical settings can be combined with plainsong, Anglican chant and motets sung by the choir. Silence is equally important during the Vigil, and a pause of at least the psalm's length is appropriate before each collect. TS provides two prayers for each reading, a traditional collect form for use with Pattern A and a *berakah* prayer for Pattern B. The former is prefaced by an optional Christological response which has the advantage of helping worshippers hear the scriptures as being read in the light of the risen Christ. If it is desired to use these, they may be said seated at the end of the silence before all stand and the president introduces the collect, which may be said or sung, with the words 'Let us pray'.

Following Pattern A, after the last of the Old Testament readings, with its psalm, silence and collect, the Easter Liturgy changes gear as the joyful singing of the *Gloria in Excelsis* approaches. An effective transition from anticipatory prophecy to canticle of praise is difficult to achieve. That TS has positioned the Easter acclamation at this point in the liturgy suggests that it can function as a bridge between the two (p. 338). There are, however, at least two difficulties with this. First, the Alleluia, following on immediately from the Amen after the collect, seems to come from nowhere like a liturgical jack-in-the-box, suggesting that the resurrection happens suddenly and unexpectedly at this point. Second, it can be more effective if the Alleluia, which has not been sung since Shrove Tuesday, returns in its normal liturgical place, after the New Testament reading, and thus heralds the proclamation of the Easter Gospel.

How, then, is this transition to be achieved? Although the fanfare which precedes the *Gloria* needs to be sudden and dramatic, it may be possible to combine this with a more gradual change of scene. For example, if there are a large number of altar candles and lamps to be lit, servers can start to light these during the psalm following the final Old Testament reading so that a rising level of light helps to raise the sense of eager anticipation among those who are soon to proclaim the resurrection of Christ with an outburst of praise and thanksgiving. As the congregation sees the candles and lamps being lit round the church, they can blow out their own hand-held candles so that their hands are free to join in the making of the joyful noise.

After the last collect there should be a short pause before the organ fanfare is sounded. At this point all the lights in the church should be put on and 'bells rung, cymbals clashed, noise made' (TS: p. 338). If party-poppers have been distributed, this is the moment to let them off and, with due consideration to health and safety, sparklers may be lit and waved! After a minute or so the *Gloria in Excelsis* begins, and may be intoned by the president. On this occasion a well-known setting in which everyone can join in is preferable to one sung by the choir alone. Bells may be rung throughout the canticle but, once it begins, people's primary attention should be focused on singing rather than making any other noise.

At the end of the *Gloria* the president sings or says the Collect of Easter Day after which all sit for the New Testament reading. Although the psalm which follows the Romans reading is optional in TS, with a triple Alleluia as its response, it may also fulfil the function of the Gospel acclamation. If used in this way, the custom of the president (or another minister or cantor) first intoning the Alleluia is to be encouraged. All stand and the president sings Alleluia three times, each time beginning on a higher note. The traditional chant can be found in *The Great Week* (Dean 1992: p. 97) but other versions may also be used. What is important is that it is clear that the

Alleluia has returned. At the end of the Alleluia the psalm begins. Verses from Psalm 118 may be used as an alternative to Psalm 114. A setting of the former, which incorporates the popular *Celtic Alleluia*, can be found in *The Great Week* (pp. 97–8).

Once the psalm has begun, the thurifer approaches the president who puts on incense and blesses it. The rest of the Gospel ceremonial is as normal, except that no acolyte candles are carried in the Gospel procession since, to quote Elliott, 'on this night, the Easter Candle suffices to honour the risen Lord in his Gospel' (Elliott 2002: p. 286).

Although it is tempting to omit the sermon at the Easter Liturgy, it is not 'almost superfluous', as Giles suggests (Giles 2008: p. 150), but should, in a few words and perhaps quite informally, draw together some of the strands of the liturgy. It can fulfil a particularly valuable function if there are candidates to be baptized and/or confirmed in making connections between what they have already experienced and what is about to happen. In some places it has become customary to read the *Easter Homily* of St John Chrysostom at this point in the liturgy, or another suitable Patristic reading.

## The Liturgy of Initiation

Whether or not there are candidates for baptism and/or confirmation, the Liturgy of Initiation begins with a procession to the font. The Roman rite suggests some words which the president may use to introduce this; or a more informal introduction, following on from the sermon, may be preferred. When there are candidates for baptism the president may say:

*President*   Dear friends in Christ,
as our brothers and sisters approach the waters of
rebirth,
let us help them by our prayers
and ask God, our almighty Father,
to support them with his mercy and love.

(SM 2005: p. 305)

Alternatively, if there are no candidates for baptism, the following may be used:

*President*    Dear friends in Christ,
let us ask God, the almighty Father,
to bless this font,
that those reborn in it
may be made one with his adopted children in Christ.

(SM 2005: p. 311)

Hand-held candles are lit and a procession to the font is formed, led by the deacon carrying the Easter Candle. Behind the deacon come any candidates for baptism (not carrying candles) and/or confirmation, the servers and ministers carrying their candles, and the president. If possible, members of the congregation should also join in this procession, with their hand-held candles, and gather round the font. If there is no room for them to leave their seats, they should at least turn to face the font.

Traditionally, the litany of saints is sung during the procession. Those who are uncomfortable with invoking the prayers of the saints may wish to use the second section from the Thanksgiving for the Resurrection (TS: p. 422) or the Thanksgiving for the Holy Ones of God (TS: pp. 558–60) with a triple Alleluia as the response (see also ALG 5, pp. 83–4).

Once at the font, the order of service will depend on whether or not there are candidates for baptism and/or confirmation. Table 3.1 lists the various options with the required elements.

If Pattern B is followed, the Presentation of the Candidates, Decision/Renewal of Baptismal Vows and Signing with the Cross may take place as part of the Service of Light (TS: pp. 352–3, note 12). Whichever pattern is used, if there are candidates for baptism and/or confirmation at the Easter Liturgy, the whole assembly makes the Decision (TS: pp. 342, 356) with them as part of their Renewal of Baptismal Vows.

Before the Prayer over the Water, water is poured into the font, either by one of the candidates, a sponsor or another member of the congregation. If possible, it should be poured in from a height so that it is clearly visible to the congregation (see CCW1: pp. 166–7). The prayer may be sung and is prefaced by two responses, after which the president's hands may be raised to the *orans* position. At the words 'Bless this water', the president may take the Easter Candle from the deacon and lower the base of it into the water, either once

Table 3.1   The Liturgy of Initiation at the Easter Vigil (Pattern A)

| *Baptism and Confirmation with Renewal of Baptismal Vows* | *Confirmation with Renewal of Baptismal Vows* |
| --- | --- |
| Presentation of the Candidates | Presentation of the Candidates (CI: p. 111) |
| Decision/Renewal of Baptismal Vows | Decision/Renewal of Baptismal Vows |
| Signing with the Cross | |
| Prayer over the Water | Prayer over the Water |
| Profession of Faith | Profession of Faith |
| Baptism | |
| Sprinkling with baptismal water | Sprinkling with baptismal water |
| Confirmation | Confirmation |
| (Commission) | (Commission) |
| Welcome | |

| *Renewal of Baptismal Vows* |
| --- |
| Renewal of Baptismal Vows |
| Prayer over the Water |
| Profession of Faith |
| Sprinkling with baptismal water |

or three times. The repeated refrain, '*Saving God*, **give us life**', is optional. If used, the response should preferably be sung, first by a cantor or choir, and then by everyone, so that the prayer can continue without the congregation's attention needing to be fixed on the order of service to find out when and what they have to sing.

The Apostles' Creed is *the* baptismal profession of faith, and this should always be used in preference to the shorter alternative formula. As with the Decision, at the Easter Liturgy it seems quite appropriate for dialogues between president and people to move at a faster pace than would normally be the case, allowing the sense of exuberant joy which burst forth before the *Gloria* to bubble up through the rest of the rite. The Easter Liturgy may often be a long service, but it should never be celebrated lugubriously. The Vigil of

Readings provides time for silence and contemplation. With the singing of the *Gloria* a new pace is set which needs to be maintained, without rushing, until the final dismissal.

If there are any candidates for baptism, they are baptized after the Profession of Faith. If they are also to be confirmed, they are not anointed with chrism during the post-baptismal prayer, 'May God, who has received you by baptism into his Church' (TS: p. 345). The sprinkling of the whole congregation with baptismal water follows, during which suitable hymns, songs and chants may be sung. ALG 5 suggests a number of chants and songs which may be sung during the sprinkling (ALG 5: pp. 59–60). In addition, G. W. Briggs' hymn 'Now is eternal life' (NEH 114) is appropriate. TS also allows for members of the congregation to approach the font and sign themselves with the water. If there are candidates for confirmation who have not just been baptized, these could be invited to sign themselves in this way, after which the president could move among the congregation, sprinkling them. Although an aspergilium could be used for this, a large sprig of rosemary is to be preferred, so that the sprinkling can be smelled as well as felt. During the sprinkling a server takes some of the blessed water in a jug and fills the stoups. At the end of the liturgy any remaining water may be put into suitable containers and used to fill the stoups during the course of the year.

TS provides two presidential texts to conclude the sprinkling. It would be appropriate to raise the hands into the *orans* position for the first. For the second, the president's hands may be extended towards the people, as if giving a solemn blessing (see ALG 3: p. 77).

If confirmation is to follow, it should be celebrated at the font rather than moving to another part of the building in the middle of the Liturgy of Initiation (the bishop standing to confirm). The Commission, which may be celebrated here or at the beginning of the Sending Out, is optional and, at the Easter Liturgy, probably best omitted altogether. If there have been candidates for baptism, the Welcome follows, leading into the Liturgy of the Eucharist.

For further discussion on the celebration of the rites of Christian Initiation, see ALG 5: pp. 101–7.

## The Liturgy of the Eucharist

With the ministers and congregation still gathered around the font, the Liturgy of the Eucharist begins with the Peace, for which TS provides appropriate texts and suggests that everyone greets each other with the words 'Christ is risen' (TS: p. 367). Hand-held candles should be extinguished at this point and, as the offertory hymn begins, the deacon carrying the Easter Candle leads the ministers to the sanctuary and puts the candle back in its stand. The gifts of bread and wine should also be carried in this procession, preferably by two people who are about to receive Holy Communion for the first time. If the Liturgy of the Eucharist is to take place in another part of the building, the whole congregation joins in the procession; if not, the people return to their places.

The Eucharist now continues in the usual way. When the president censes the altar, the Paschal Candle may also be censed with three double swings (see ALG 3: p. 31). During the Eucharistic Prayer, the extended preface with its reference to 'this night of our redemption' is particularly appropriate (TS: p. 368). If Prayer G is used, TS suggests a petition for the newly baptized and confirmed which might be included (p. 333). Although such a petition is entirely appropriate, Prayer G cannot be used with an extended or short preface.

After Communion the Blessed Sacrament is restored to the tabernacle or aumbry. If it is desired to highlight this moment, it could take place after the Prayer after Communion. An acolyte may accompany the deacon or another minister who carries the sacrament from the altar. As they approach the tabernacle or aumbry, a fanfare may be sounded and bells rung. As the sacrament is restored, the president and congregation may join in the Easter acclamation, after which the final hymn may be sung and, if desired, the congregation's candles re-lit. During the hymn, if there are any newly baptized, they should gather with one of the ministers near the Easter Candle.

If the Easter acclamation has already been used, the president may preface the blessing with the ordinary greeting (see ALG 3: p. 77). Baptism candles, lit from the Easter Candle, are given to the newly baptized and the liturgy concludes with the dismissal sung, if possible, by the deacon using the form provided in TS or, more simply, 'Go in the peace of Christ. Alleluia, alleluia' (p. 371).

The procession forms up in the usual way with the acolytes and processional cross leading. Those who have been baptized or confirmed may walk with the ministers, and the congregation may follow them out of the church. Depending on the timing of the liturgy, a celebratory party and/or breakfast accompanied by fireworks may follow.

## Worship on Easter Day

When a community has already celebrated the Easter Liturgy, the Eucharist of Easter Day should, ritually speaking, be a relatively straightforward affair. If an Easter Garden has been set up in the church, the entrance procession may make a station at it. The entrance hymn may be broken and the Prayers at the Easter Garden (TS: p. 419) used. If the garden is to be blessed, the *berakah* prayer may be adapted as follows:

> + *Bless this garden, and grant that we who have*
> *prepared it*
> in celebration of his victory
> may be strengthened in faith,
> know the power of his presence,
> and rejoice in the hope of eternal glory.

The garden may then be sprinkled with baptismal water and censed. The Prayers of Penitence may take place here or in their usual position as part of the Gathering. *Kyrie* Confession B2 (TS: p. 429) is suggested.

CW provides Easter Day readings for each of the liturgical years. In the Roman rite the Easter Sequence, *Victimae Paschali*, is sung after the second reading. A version of this may be found at NEH 519 and in DP: p. 640.

In churches where the Easter Liturgy has not been celebrated, and members of the congregation have not joined in its celebration elsewhere, TS provides an order for a Mid-Morning Eucharist on Easter Day using Elements from the Easter Liturgy (pp. 401–3). Although this service omits some of the elements from the Service of Light (such as the fire), ceremonial from the Paschal Vigil can easily be adapted to meet the requirements of this celebration. The same is true for the material from the Service of Light which is included in the outline Service of the Word on Easter Day (TS: pp. 404–7).

# 4

# Eastertide

And now we give you thanks
because in his victory over the grave a new age has dawned,
the long reign of sin is ended,
a broken world is being renewed
and humanity is once again made whole.

(Short preface for Eastertide, TS: p. 436)

## Liturgical character

The fundamental, non-negotiable aspect of the Easter season is, of course, 'joy'. Whereas in Lent there was a distinct anticipatory thread of this, it was rightly subdued, but at and after Easter it should be released with unqualified and unambiguous commitment, and the celebration of the liturgy should reflect this. More specifically, early Christianity viewed the period after Easter as a time of rejoicing in the presence of the Bridegroom, i.e. the risen Christ. Although the unity of the 50 days was later obscured by the emergence of the Easter Octave and the period around the Ascension, the importance of the single season, 'a single festival period' (TS: p. 427), is now re-emphasized, as reflected in the rubrics of CW. The 50-day season is marked by the repeated use of the 'Alleluia' which returns at the Easter Vigil. Decoration of the church returns in abundance and vestments are the best white and gold. As the Introduction to the Easter Vigil in TS notes of that occasion, 'all the resources of the church – music, flowers, bells, colours – are used to celebrate Christ's resurrection' (TS: p. 323), and this ought to be the case throughout the following season. The Easter Candle should be prominent, and lit for every service.

Despite the overall unity of the single season, however, liturgically it can be seen as two periods which each contribute to the celebration of the significance of Christ's victory. The first is the 40 days from Easter to Ascension, which reflects on the resurrection itself. In the second, much shorter ten-day section from Ascension to Pentecost, the consequences of the victory are celebrated – Christ ascending to his Father to reign always and everywhere, and looking towards the promised and concomitant gift of the Holy Spirit to the nascent Church. The way in which the plentiful material for the season (TS: pp. 427–502) is organized recognizes both the ongoing character of the season as a whole and the liturgical implications of the specific 'summits' of the Ascension and Pentecost towards its end. The material also includes resources for the Stations of the Resurrection.

## The Eucharist in Eastertide – Easter to Ascension

The principal Sunday Eucharist in Eastertide should consciously continue the liturgical character begun at the Easter Vigil. The first section of the TS material contains seasonal material for use from Easter until the Ascension (TS: pp. 428–42).

### The Gathering

TS has a rubric at the head of this material (TS: p. 428) which encourages the prayers of penitence to be led from the Easter Garden during the season. If this is taken up, it has implications for the Gathering. The ministers may either enter as the organ plays and proceed directly to the Easter Garden by the shortest route, or the first part of a hymn may be sung as they do so, the rest after the station at the garden. If the garden is visible from the main body of the church, the people could simply turn to face it as the ministers arrive there. If it isn't visible, the people could gather around the garden. While not explicitly stated in the rubric, the liturgical greeting (and the Easter greeting) must still be given before the penitential rite. The rite can be followed by a hymn (rather than singing a hymn at the entry) as the ministers go to their places to continue the service, the people following if they have gathered around the garden.

It would be possible and very appropriate to the season if the penitential rite included sprinkling – this could take place at the Easter

Garden, or a station could be made at the font. Indeed the font (assuming it is at or near the west end of the church) might well be an alternative starting point in any case for the liturgy in Eastertide, the greeting, penitential rite and sprinkling taking place there rather than at the Easter Garden. Here too, the ministers could go to the font as the organ plays, and the people either turn to face the font or gather around it as they arrive, joining the procession after the penitential rite. The TS 'Act of Penitence' (p. 430) can be used. This refers to the president praying 'over a vessel of water'. It is best if this vessel is the font, although the layout of the church building may suggest that a separate vessel placed prominently at the head of the nave is more visibly appropriate. During the sprinkling 'suitable hymns, songs or anthems may be sung' (TS: p. 430). These might include the *vidi aquam*, for which see the material for the Baptism of Christ (TS: p. 176, and ALG 5: pp. 57–8). However, the sprinkling should not be excessively prolonged – in a small church or if the people are gathered around the font, there will be no need for the president to move while sprinkling them. Another option would be for the president to sprinkle the people as the ministers move up the nave, saying the suggested absolution (or another authorized one) on arrival at the chair.

A hymn could be sung after the penitential rite as the ministers alone or with the people process up the centre to their places. Alternatively, this procession could take place as the *Gloria in Excelsis* is sung, all arriving in their places for the collect. The altar could also be censed before the collect if desired.

If the option of beginning at the font (and perhaps with sprinkling) is adopted, the second of the three invitations to confession would be appropriate: 'In baptism we died with Christ . . .' (TS: p. 428).

However the service is begun (and it may begin in the usual way with an entrance hymn, the ministers processing to their places, the altar censed, etc.), the greeting must be accompanied by the Easter greeting (*not* replaced by it, as ASB directed), e.g.:

*President*    In the name of the Father,
            and of the Son,
            and of the + Holy Spirit.

*All*        **Amen.**

| *President* | The Lord be with you |
| *All* | **and also with you.** |

| *President* | Alleluia. Christ is risen. |
| *All* | **He is risen indeed. Alleluia.** |

The shorter greeting ('The Lord be with you') is preferable for use with the Easter greeting. The *Gloria in Excelsis* must be sung on Sundays during Eastertide.

## The Liturgy of the Word

It is best that three readings and the psalmody provided by the Lectionary are used. These must include the reading from the Acts of the Apostles. If three readings are not possible, the reading from the Acts of the Apostles should be chosen as the reading before the Gospel. If Morning Prayer is celebrated before the Sung Eucharist, the Old Testament reading set for the Eucharist could be read at it as the single reading. A Gospel acclamation (TS: p. 431) should be used before the Gospel. The five texts in TS are reproduced in DEL (p. 816), and could indeed also be used at weekday celebrations of the Eucharist in Eastertide.

In Eastertide it would be appropriate to underscore the baptismal emphasis by the use of the Apostles' Creed on Sundays in place of the Nicene Creed or other authorized Affirmation of Faith.

## The Liturgy of the Sacrament

There are no unique features of this part of the liturgy apart from the usual need to select variable texts from the seasonal provision of Introductions to the Peace (with Alleluias) (TS: p. 435), Prayers at the Preparation of the Table (TS: p. 435) and short and extended prefaces (TS: pp. 436–7). The final preface is responsive in form, and based on 1 Corinthians 15. In that it does not address God throughout, it is of a different order from any other CW preface, and indeed would seem to step outside the Western tradition for the genre in addressing 'death' rhetorically as Paul does. For the giving of Communion, the form 'The body/blood of Christ keep you in eternal life'

(CWMV: p. 295) is particularly appropriate to the season and has baptismal resonances.

## The Dismissal

Of the options supplied (TS: pp. 438–9), the final, solemn form of blessing is recommended for use on Sundays in Eastertide. The others may be used varyingly at weekday celebrations of the Eucharist and on other occasions.

Following the form established in TS for other occasions, there is provision for an Alternative Dismissal. An acclamation is followed by a Dismissal Gospel (John 11.25–26), and the solemn blessing (TS: p. 439).

There are five dismissal texts (TS: p. 440), also for use when the Alternative Dismissal form is not employed, although the following simple form (sung if possible) would suffice:

*Deacon/President*   Go in the peace of Christ. Alleluia, alleluia.
*All*                **Thanks be to God. Alleluia, alleluia.**

An Easter dismissal text should be used throughout the season up to and including the Day of Pentecost.

## Stations of the Resurrection

Many Christians commit considerable time and effort to the liturgical observance of Lent. Sadly, such devotion is rarely matched in Eastertide. In some ways this is not surprising. The Holy Week journey can sometimes be such a demanding experience that, at the end of Easter Day, there is often very little enthusiasm for embarking on another lengthy seasonal celebration which requires participative engagement and commitment.

The Stations of the Resurrection, a parallel observance to the Way of the Cross, enables individuals and communities to focus on the mystery of the resurrection and the appearances of the risen Christ in a structured way which, like its Lenten counterpart, is enhanced by visual stimulus and movement. Much of what has already been said about the Stations of the Cross can also be applied to this stational liturgy (pp. 17–24).

As TS indicates, the Stations of the Resurrection emerged relatively recently, in the second half of the last century, and was first
celebrated in Spain and Portugal (p. 443). Known as *Via Lucis* (the
Way of Light) in the Roman Catholic Church, it was officially com-
mended as a 'pious exercise' as recently as 2001. Like John Paul II's
1991 sequence of Stations of the Cross, the Stations of the Resurrection are all biblical. There is no fixed number, but TS includes 19,
beginning with the earthquake in the Matthean account of the
resurrection and concluding with the conversion of Paul on the
Damascus road.

While broadly maintaining the sequence in which the stations
appear in TS, it is unlikely that it would be desirable to use all of
them on any one occasion. Indeed, a suitable choice of stations over
the weeks between Easter Day and Pentecost may assist both individuals and communities to sustain their celebration of the resurrection
throughout the 50 days. As with the Way of the Cross, in some places
they may form part of a Sunday evening service. Elsewhere, they
might be used on a weekday, perhaps forming the Liturgy of the
Word within a celebration of the Eucharist. TS once again gives
guidance as to how such a liturgy could be ordered and points to the
rubrics relating to A Service of the Word with a Celebration of Holy
Communion (CWMV: p. 25). In Eastertide it would be appropriate
for sprinkling with baptismal water to be included within the penitential rite (TS: p. 430). The Eucharist could begin at the font and
the order shown in Table 4.1 could be used.

Unless the Stations of the Resurrection is celebrated within the
context of a Eucharist, there is no requirement for a priest or deacon
to preside. If the officiant is ordained, a cotta or surplice and white
stole may be worn and, if desired, a white cope. In addition to lighting altar candles, the Easter Candle should also be lit for this service,
and may lead the procession round the stations instead of a cross
and lights. It may be carried by a server, or members of the congregation could take it in turns to carry it.

Unlike the Stations of the Cross, there are very few places which
are likely to have their own images of the Stations of the Resurrection. Although resources are gradually becoming more readily
available, not least in electronic format, in many cases it will be up
to individual communities to design their own. For example, one
or more of the opening stations could take place at the Easter

**Table 4.1   Order for Stations of the Resurrection**

| CW Order One (2000) | Stations of the Resurrection (2006) |
| --- | --- |
| **The Gathering** | |
| Trinitarian Invocation | |
| Greeting | |
| Easter Acclamation | |
| | Sentences |
| | Introduction |
| Act of Penitence (TS: p. 430) | |
| Collect | |
| **Liturgy of the Word** | |
| | Stations of the Resurrection |
| **Liturgy of the Sacrament** | |
| Offertory | |
| Eucharistic Prayer | |
| Lord's Prayer | |
| Breaking of the Bread | |
| Giving of Communion (Easter form, CWMV: p. 180) | |
| Prayer after Communion (the prayer for Easter 5, CWMV: p. 403, is appropriate) | |
| **Dismissal** | |
| | Responsory |
| | Blessing |
| | Peace |

Garden and/or in a churchyard; an altar could be used for the sixth station, the Road to Emmaus; the procession could move outside and the congregation encouraged to look upwards as they hear the disciples being asked, 'Men of Galilee, why do you stand looking up towards heaven?' (Acts 1.11); and as the tongues of flame descend at Pentecost, red lamps could be distributed as a focus for prayer and which, at the end of the service, could be left around the Easter Garden, or in another suitable place. *Together for a Season* suggests ways in which children may be involved in designing stations and the whole liturgy used as an all-age celebration (Ambrose 2007: pp. 228–38).

## The Gathering

Organ music, or even suitable recorded music, is appropriate as people gather for the service. A bowl of incense may burn near the Easter Garden. As with the Way of the Cross, the minister may stand before the altar, or in another central place, to introduce the rite. TS concludes the Gathering and every station with one of the memorial acclamations from the Eucharistic Prayers:

*All*        **Dying you destroyed our death,**
              **rising you restored our life:**
              **Lord Jesus, come in glory.**

This is an optional text, so if its use after every station is thought to be too repetitious, some of the traditional texts associated with the Way of the Cross (Lord's Prayer, *Gloria Patri* and Hail Mary) may be used. Alternatively the Easter acclamation or another of the memorial acclamations (**Christ has died. Christ is risen. Christ will come again**) would be appropriate.

## Stations

Each station begins with a versicle and response based on John 11.25–26. If it is customary to genuflect or make a profound bow at the beginning of each station of the cross, it would seem logical to repeat that action with each station of the resurrection. Each station may also be announced in the same way. At the end of each section, a verse or verses from a suitable Easter hymn may be sung as the procession moves to the next station.

## Conclusion

The structure of the conclusion is identical to that for the Stations of the Cross, except that the Peace is exchanged at the end of the service, thus encouraging an informal end to the rite. Alternatively, after the last station, the service may end with Eucharistic devotions and Benediction.

# Ascension Day

The marking of Ascension Day is an important element in the unfolding theology of the resurrection. It is an integral part of Eastertide, yet takes the victory of Christ literally to yet greater heights and yet wider consequences. He who has risen 'triumphant from the grave', as the Exsultet at the Easter Vigil puts it (TS: p. 337), now ascends to reign for ever at the right hand of the Father so that 'where he is, we might thither ascend' (TS: p. 478). This new dimension should be marked with continuing joy and distinctive liturgical expression. The Easter Candle continues to be lit and prominently positioned at all services until and including Pentecost.

The Ascension should ideally be celebrated on Ascension Day, always the Thursday in the sixth week of the Easter season, despite the recent decision by the Roman Catholic Church in England and Wales to move Ascension Day to the following Sunday. There is a careful and distinct progression in the days following Ascension Day up to the Day of Pentecost that is reflected in calendar, lectionary and liturgical material in TS, and of which the Sunday after the Ascension (Easter 7) is an important part (see notes on this period on p. 98).

In token of the importance of the day, TS supplies a fully worked out scheme for the Eucharist (pp. 469–81).

## The Gathering

A slightly enhanced form of the Gathering is suggested: preference is given to an anthem, but a hymn can easily be substituted, and indeed might be accompanied by a procession (compare All Saints in ALG 5: pp. 80–1). 'Hail the day that sees him rise' (NEH 130), or the Ascension Day version of 'Hail thee, Festival Day' (NEH 109) are possibilities. The suggested versicle and response (TS: p. 470) could be sung at the conclusion of the procession, rather as *The English Hymnal* suggested for such an occasion, 'at the Sanctuary step' (EH: p. 817). For processions in general see ALG 5 (pp. 19–21).

The liturgical greeting follows, and here the 'Grace, mercy and peace . . .' version is suggested. There is no Easter greeting at this point if the 'Ascension Reading' is used (but see below), but if it is not, the Easter greeting should immediately follow. There is a supplied introductory text for the president, in line with other major liturgies, and as on those other occasions it may be replaced by 'other suitable words'. If the 'Ascension Reading' which follows in the TS order is omitted, the end of the set text will need to be modified since it invites 'let us hear the story of his parting' (TS: p. 470).

Mirroring the Palm Gospel on Palm Sunday, an 'Ascension Reading' is provided (Acts 1.4–11). This is in fact one of those provided in the Lectionary, the suggestion being that it may be used immediately after the introduction, before the *Gloria in Excelsis*. The Prayers of Penitence have been omitted entirely. However if it is desired to retain them, the Acts reading could simply be read during the Liturgy of the Word with the other lections, and penitential texts selected from the Ascension to Pentecost seasonal material (TS: pp. 483–4). If the suggested order is followed, the Ascension Reading should not be read 'by the person leading this part of the service' (TS: p. 471), i.e. the president. In TS, however, the reader (whoever he or she may be) is to give the Easter greeting at the end of the reading: this is normally a presidential text used at the beginning of the liturgy, so its use here is rather odd. It also refers technically to the resurrected Christ, whereas its use here would seem to be in reference specifically to the Christ who has ascended – the resurrection is not mentioned in Acts 1.4–11. Then, however, 'a minister may say' a text from the letter to the Hebrews: 'Seeing we have a great high priest who has passed into the heavens . . .' (TS: p. 471) as what seems to be an introduction to the *Gloria*. In the circumstances this could well be a diaconal text, but equally (and perhaps preferably) a presidential one. In view of these confusions, the following order can be adopted:

- In the name of the Father ...
- Greeting.
- Easter acclamation.
- Introduction.
- Acts reading (read by any person) concluding with 'This is the word of the Lord' and its response.
- Sentence (TS: p. 471) said by the president.

While TS makes the *Gloria* optional (p. 471), since this is a Principal Feast it ought not to be omitted.

## The Liturgy of the Word

'If the Acts reading has already been used, only one reading from Scripture precedes the Gospel reading' (TS: p. 473). This rubric seems to confirm that the omission of the 'Ascension Reading' from the Gathering might be legitimate. If so omitted, it should certainly be read here. The canticle should be sung if possible. The first Gospel Acclamation is from the Ascension to Pentecost seasonal material. After the Gospel and Sermon the first of the two forms of intercession for Ascension Day (TS: pp. 475–6) might itself be used between Ascension Day and Pentecost since it specifically includes 'seeking the Father's blessing and the gifts of the Spirit' (TS: p. 475), although it is not included in the seasonal material for that period. Despite the TS rubric directing the Nicene Creed (p. 474), if the Apostles' Creed is being said throughout Eastertide it ought to be used here too (a similar course of action being recommended for Pentecost, where this rubric also appears).

## The Liturgy of the Sacrament

The extended and short prefaces provided are unique to Ascension Day (TS: p. 478) and one of them should be used. There are also unique texts for the Breaking of the Bread and the Invitation to Communion (TS: p. 479), the latter having as an alternative the Easter form of the invitation in CWMV (p. 180). For the giving of Communion, the form 'the bread of heaven in Jesus Christ' would be suitable for this day when the reign of the Christ 'who has passed into the heavens', who feeds us with 'the bread of heaven' and gives us 'a foretaste of the heavenly banquet' (Prayers after Communion, TS: p. 479) is a particular liturgical focus.

## The Dismissal

There is a longer form of dismissal (pp. 480–1) similar in nature to the TS 'Dismissal Gospel' but which looks forward to the gift of the Spirit at Pentecost by a reading from Acts (1.12–14). This mirrors the 'Ascension Reading' at the beginning of the liturgy (when used). After the Responsory, which could be sung, either silence or a 'reflective hymn' is suggested. The Taizé chant 'Veni, sancte Spiritus' is appropriate, and could be continued softly while the solemn blessing (p. 481) is given. It would be possible then to continue the reflective, expectant mood by choosing appropriately subdued music to be played after the dismissal.

## Ascension to Pentecost

It is important in this short period of ten days both to maintain the joy of the continuing Easter season while also acknowledging the consequences of the Ascension and the expectancy which is appropriate to the coming Day of Pentecost. As these ten days (including the Seventh Sunday of Easter) are still part of Eastertide, white is used as the liturgical colour, even though the liturgical focus shifts towards prayer for the coming of the Spirit. The liturgical material in TS (pp. 483–90) attempts to strike this balance, though tipping in overall favour of Pentecost (and is included in the Pentecost section), but it needs to be accompanied by careful choices of hymns and other elements. The Easter Candle continues to be visible and lit at all services. Festivals falling during this period should be observed in the normal way, but it may be appropriate to commemorate Lesser Festivals more simply than usual, with a mention in the prayers of intercession only, rather than a proper collect and readings.

# Pentecost

Pentecost (the 'fiftieth' day) is not a season, but a Principal Feast which marks the culmination of the celebration of the resurrection as, in fulfilment of Christ's promise, the Holy Spirit is outpoured upon the disciples. After Easter Day itself, this is the second most important festival in the Christian year and the birthday of the Church. Once also a focus for holidays and festivities in the wider community, though these have been maintained in some places (for example, Whit Walks in Lancashire), Whitsun has, by and large, very little significance in the secular world. This, if nothing else, should incite the Christian community to make this celebration a significant and joyful occasion in the life of the Church.

The Roman rite provides a full set of propers for a Vigil Mass of Pentecost. Where it is desired to celebrate the Eucharist before or after the first Evening Prayer of Pentecost, the following readings may be used with the Pentecost collect and prayer after Communion:

> Genesis 11.1–9 *or* Exodus 19.3–8, 16–20 *or* Ezekiel 37.1–14 *or*
> Joel 3.1–5
> Psalm 104.1–2, 26, 29–32
> Romans 8.22–27
> John 7.37–39.

## Liturgy of the Feast of Pentecost

TS provides a fully worked out form of service for the Eucharist on this Principal Feast. Red is the liturgical colour and the Easter Candle should be lit. If anointing is to take place as part of the Prayer for Personal Renewal, the oil of chrism may be carried in the entrance procession and placed in a position where it is clearly visible to the congregation, perhaps with a small red votive light burning next to it. If possible, the oil should be contained in a glass cruet, or similar vessel, rather than in a silver stock. If hand-held candles are to be lit from the Easter Candle as part of the Dismissal, these should be distributed as people arrive. Before the service, rather than the organ playing, a simple chant invoking the Spirit, such as 'Veni, sancte Spiritus' from the Taizé community, may be sung quietly to help people prepare for the service. On this occasion, it would be particularly appropriate for the president and other ministers to prepare themselves with the congregation by kneeling in a suitable place, such as in front of the altar or in a side chapel (see also ALG 3: pp. 23–4).

## The Gathering

The Gathering begins in the usual way. If incense is used, it would be appropriate to cense the Easter Candle as well as the altar (see also ALG 3: p. 31). TS provides words of introduction which are said after the greeting and Easter acclamation (p. 491). For the responsory which follows, which prays for the indwelling of the Spirit, it may be appropriate for people to kneel, including the ministers, who may kneel in front of the altar. Instead of the responsory (p. 492), the Spirit may be invoked in the words of the ancient Pentecost hymn *Veni creator* (NEH 138 or DP: pp. 284–5) which, if not used here, should, if possible, be sung at some point during the celebration. After a period of silence which, depending on the composition of the congregation, could last for several minutes, the people stand for the Pentecost Reading. If not read here, it must be used during the Liturgy of the Word, but there is something to be said for setting the scene for the whole service and preparing for the Prayer for Personal Renewal, if it is to follow, by reading the account of the first Christian Pentecost as part of the Gathering. Although it is not customary to stand for a non-Gospel reading, since Acts 2 provides the biblical account of the event which is the focus for this celebration, this posture seems appropriate. Giles suggests that the reading's reference to the several languages in which the message was heard can be easily reproduced in many multicultural communities (Giles 2008: p. 176). While being sensitive to ethnic and racial issues, the reading could effectively be divided between two or three people, each reading in their first language.

The Prayer for Personal Renewal is optional but seems entirely suitable on this occasion and may also help to raise the profile of the ministry of anointing (see also ALG 4: pp. 49–50). After the reading it would be appropriate for a member of the congregation, perhaps a lay member of the ministry team or someone who attended the Chrism Eucharist, to bring the oil to the president. It is preferable to use the oil of chrism, if the church has it, rather than to bless oil specifically for the occasion, especially if the oils were received into church at the beginning of the Eucharist of the Last Supper on Maundy Thursday. If chrism is used, the words of presentation may be changed to make this clear:

> The oil of chrism, blessed by the Bishop,
> for the renewal of God's people.

However, if oil is to be blessed, a prayer is provided which, since it follows the CW convention of asking that God's blessing 'rest upon those anointed with this oil in your name' (TS: p. 493) rather than on the oil itself, may be considered suitable even when chrism is used. Strangely, TS gives no guidance as to how, where or by whom the anointing should be administered, other than it may be accompanied by appropriate hymns and songs. In part, the answers to these questions will depend on how many people seek this ministry. In larger congregations where a significant proportion of worshippers are likely to come forward, several stations may be set up in different parts of the church. Otherwise people may come forward as they would for Holy Communion, or go to side chapels if there are any. Since, in other CW rites, anointing is restricted to the clergy, it is probably best to follow that practice here, although lay members of a ministry team could be involved in the laying on of hands, if that is also used as part of the ministry of prayer. It should be made clear that children as well as adults are welcome to be anointed. If children normally leave the assembly early on in the service and return during the Liturgy of the Sacrament, on this occasion it would be appropriate for them to stay at least until they have been anointed. As to how the anointing should be administered, since God's people are being equipped and empowered for service, it may be appropriate to anoint the palms of the hands with the sign of the cross as well as or instead of the forehead. The whole congregation, sitting or kneeling, should be encouraged to pray for those coming forward, as well as for themselves. At the end of the rite a server with a lavabo may need to wash the hands of the ministers of anointing. The president's Trinitarian acclamation and its response provide a useful cue for the congregation to stand for the *Gloria in Excelsis* which follows. The Gathering concludes with the collect.

## The Liturgy of the Word and Sacrament

After a rather lengthy Gathering, there is something to be said for the Liturgy of the Word being somewhat shorter than normal. If the Acts reading has already been used, the Liturgy of the Word begins with the Epistle (it would be odd to read the Old Testament reading having heard the account of Pentecost in Acts) and may be followed immediately by a Gospel acclamation (the triple 'Alleluia' is particularly appropriate on this festival) and the proclamation of the Gospel. The Roman rite directs that the sequence 'Veni, sancte Spiritus' should be sung on this feast (after the second reading). If it is desired to include this, a version can be found at NEH 520 and in DP (p. 642).

A suggested form of intercession is provided which may be followed by Prayers of Penitence. Although the Gathering does not include any explicitly penitential material, penitence should form part of any prayer for personal renewal, and so it seems unnecessary to include further penitential material here.

The service continues with the Liturgy of the Sacrament, for which TS suggests appropriate texts, including an extended and short preface and introductory words for the Lord's Prayer (p. 499).

## The Dismissal

The Dismissal is a distinctive feature of this rite and consists of a *berakah* prayer, offered next to the Easter Candle, which gives thanks that the 'flame of heaven' now 'rests on every believer' (p. 501), the lighting of the congregation's hand-held candles, a commission to 'live out what you proclaim' and a procession outside, or to the back of the church, for the blessing and dismissal. Although TS suggests that the Easter Candle may be extinguished after the commission (if there are no other services that day), there is something to be said for the light of the risen Christ leading God's people out into the world. Since the Easter Candle will remain at the font until it is renewed the following Easter, it is also appropriate that its movement from altar to font should be marked liturgically, a practice which Elliott also commends (Elliott 2002: pp. 162–3).

The following is an example of one way in which the rite might

conclude. Facing the Easter Candle, the president says the thanksgiving prayer with hands in the *orans* position, bringing them together
at the doxology. Another minister, possibly a deacon, assistant priest
or Reader, then lifts the candle out of its stand and moves to a central
position. The servers, choir and congregation approach to light their
hand-held candles from it. During this, an appropriate chant or song
may be sung and, if incense is used, the president puts some into the
thurible and blesses it, ready for the procession. After all the candles
have been lit, the president lights his or her own candle and stands
next to the Easter Candle to lead the commission.

In TS the Conclusion includes a reference to the Spirit driving 'us
out into the wild places of the world'. There are several reasons why
this may be considered inappropriate, not least because it suggests
too great a distinction between Church and world (see also CCW2:
p. 101). The TS text may be adapted as follows:

| | |
|---|---|
| *President* | The Lord is here. |
| *All* | **His Spirit is with us.** |

| | |
|---|---|
| *President* | Today we have remembered the coming of God's power on the disciples and we invite that same Spirit to send us out into the world. |

| | |
|---|---|
| *Deacon/*<br>*Minister* | Let us go forth in peace. |

| | |
|---|---|
| *All* | **+ In the name of Christ. Amen.** |

The procession then moves outside or towards the font as a hymn is
sung. Something which refers to the Church's mission, such as 'We
have a Gospel to proclaim' (NEH 486) would be particularly appropriate. If incense is used, the thurifer should lead the procession,
followed by the minister carrying the Easter Candle, acolytes, other
servers, the choir, ministers and congregation. As the Easter Candle
symbolizes the presence of the risen Christ, there is no need for a cross
or crucifix to be carried. When all are gathered at the baptistery
or outside, the president may cense the Easter Candle (Elliott 2002:
p. 163) before giving the blessing. The deacon, another minister or

the president then gives the dismissal. As this is the last occasion when the double 'Alleluia' will be used, it is particularly appropriate for the dismissal to be sung. If there are no other liturgical celebrations on this feast, the candle should be left at the font.

# 5

# Trinity to All Saints

And now we give you thanks
because you have revealed the glory of your eternal fellowship
   of love with your Son and with the Holy Spirit,
three persons equal in majesty, undivided in splendour,
yet one God,
ever to be worshipped and adored.

(Short preface for Trinity Sunday, TS: p. 509)

## Liturgical character

The period from Trinity Sunday to All Saints comprises the largest part of Ordinary Time, but includes several occasions that have particular liturgical forms and opportunities. Aside from these, the regular round of Sundays after Trinity must not be forgotten. In a rather indifferent poem, 'After Trinity', John Meade Faulkner alluded to the temptation to characterize this period as the response to a kind of liturgical exhaustion:

> We have done with dogma and divinity,
>    Easter and Whitsun past,
> The long, long Sundays after Trinity
>    Are with us at last;
> The passionless Sundays after Trinity,
>    Neither feast-day nor fast.
>
> Christmas comes with plenty,
>    Lent spreads out its pall,
> But these are five and twenty,
>    The longest Sundays of all;
> The placid Sundays after Trinity,
>    Wheat-harvest, fruit-harvest, Fall.
> (Larkin 1973: pp. 40–1)

However, as Elliott remarks:

> The year of the Church settles into the time of growth, the Season of the Year sometimes called 'Ordinary Time'. But this longest phase of the year of grace is in no sense 'ordinary'. The dignity of Sunday . . . is meant to shine forth, prolonging the joy of Easter and Pentecost, to celebrate the whole mystery of Christ.
>
> (Elliott 2002: p. 167)

And John Keble, famously: 'the trivial round, the common task/ should furnish all we ought to ask' (NEH 238). In fact, though, the period from Trinity to All Saints contains several important and specific liturgical opportunities, material for which is provided by TS and described below.

## Trinity Sunday

Rather than being concerned with events in the history of salvation, Trinity Sunday is entirely focused on the theological mystery of the triune God, and therefore liturgically does not commemorate an occasion but celebrates this mystery. Historically it became a particularly popular occasion after its relatively late tenth-century origin, especially in England.

Trinity Sunday needs to be distinctive, although it has no unique ceremonies of its own. Therefore a procession would be appropriate, with the hymn 'I bind unto myself today' (St Patrick's Breastplate), or 'The God of Abraham praise'. Both of these are fairly long, so the traditional 'figure of eight' procession inside the church, or perhaps even a procession around the outside of the church (but beginning inside) is probably best, at a suitably steady pace (see ALG 5: pp. 19–20).

TS provides the usual directory of material for use on Trinity Sunday (pp. 506–13).

# The Day of Thanksgiving for the Institution of Holy Communion (Corpus Christi)

The Day of Thanksgiving for the Institution of Holy Communion, known more commonly as Corpus Christi (Body of Christ), falls on the Thursday after Trinity Sunday. Although there is some overlap between Corpus Christi and the Eucharist of the Lord's Supper on Maundy Thursday, Corpus Christi is much more festive in nature and, without the ceremonies of footwashing, stripping of the altars and the watch of the passion with which the Triduum begins, has thanksgiving for the Eucharist as its principal focus.

Categorized in the ASB as simply a 'Day of Prayer and Thanksgiving', CW permits the observance of Corpus Christi as a Festival. As such, if another Festival, such as St Barnabas (11 June), falls on the same day, Corpus Christi takes precedence and is observed on the Thursday, with the other Festival being transferred to the next available day (TS: p. 27). Since 2007 the Roman Catholic Church in England and Wales has celebrated the Solemnity of the Body and Blood of Christ on the First Sunday after Trinity. Transferring the feast in this way certainly raises the profile of Corpus Christi within the calendar and is likely to enable a larger proportion of the worshipping community to celebrate it than is possible on a weekday. Notwithstanding these advantages, there is still much to be said for a Thursday celebration, particularly if it provides the opportunity for a number of parishes to combine to celebrate it together.

On whichever day it is celebrated, some may prefer to use the Roman Catholic three-year lectionary provision, rather than the one-year scheme which CW provides. Table 5.1 sets out the three-year cycle, with the CW readings indicated in bold type.

Although now more widely observed than previously by churches and cathedrals that would not identify themselves within the Catholic tradition of the Church of England, it is still the case that, with a few exceptions, a sung celebration of the Eucharist on this feast, with a procession of the host and Benediction of the Blessed Sacrament, is only likely to be found in communities with a definite Catholic tradition. For many Anglicans, such a liturgical devotion will be a ritual and theological step too far. That said, for many churches a Eucharistic procession, particularly if it can take place outside, allows those who follow Christ to take part in a public act of

Table 5.1   Three-year cycle of readings for Corpus Christi (CW readings in bold type)

| Year A | Year B | Year C |
| --- | --- | --- |
| Deuteronomy 8.2–3, 14b–16a | Exodus 24.3–8 | **Genesis 14.18–20** |
| Psalm 147.13–16, 20–21 | **Psalm 116.10–11, 13–16** | Psalm 110.1–4 |
| 1 Corinthians 10.16–17 | Hebrews 9.11–15 | **1 Corinthians 11.23–26** |
| **John 6.51–58** | Mark 14.12–16, 22–26 | Luke 9.11–17 |

witness and worship in which they recommit themselves to being partners with God in his mission to the world.

TS provides a selection of texts which may be used rather than a fully worked out order (pp. 514–20). White is the liturgical colour for this Festival and, in some places, it will be appropriate to use the church's best white or gold vestments. In addition to the usual preparations for the Eucharist, if the rite is to conclude with a procession and Benediction, a white cope and humeral veil should be put out and a second thurible and canopy made ready in a suitable place, if they are to be used. An empty monstrance, covered with a plain white veil, is placed on the credence table or somewhere nearby. The host which will be placed in the monstrance should be consecrated at this Eucharist and not taken from the tabernacle. Before the service it should be put on the paten or in a ciborium. Alternatively, it may be consecrated in the clip or lunette that will be used in the monstrance. Hand-held candles should be given to the congregation as they arrive, and also placed ready for choir, servers and other ministers. If the procession is to go outside, lanterns should be carried instead of the normal acolyte candles.

## Gathering, Liturgy of the Word and Liturgy of the Sacrament

The Eucharist follows the normal form, making appropriate use of the texts in TS. The *Gloria in Excelsis* is sung and, if Corpus Christi is being observed as a Principal Feast (the CW equivalent of the Roman Catholic 'Solemnity'), the Creed should be said. If musical resources permit, a version of the Corpus Christi sequence, *Lauda Sion* (NEH 521), may be sung after the second reading.

## Eucharistic procession and Benediction

An understanding of the people of God as a pilgrim people journeying with the Lord needs to inform the way in which the Eucharistic procession is celebrated as well as what route it might take. All those who are able to take part in the procession should be encouraged to follow the Sacrament and, where possible, they should leave the church building and go outside, possibly even to another place of worship for Benediction.

During the administration of Communion fresh charcoal is placed in the thurible(s), and the canopy, if used, is prepared. It has become customary for children to scatter rose petals in front of the Sacrament during the procession. As Elliott suggests, it is particularly appropriate for those who have recently been admitted to Holy Communion to participate in this way (Elliott 1995: p. 257). Also during Communion, the monstrance should be placed on the altar, sideways on, next to the corporal, and the altar book and anything else removed, so that only the host to be used in the procession remains. The ablutions should take place at the credence table or in a side chapel and all the hand-held candles lit.

If possible, the president should be assisted by two other ministers, one on either side, for the procession and Benediction. After Communion, one of the assistant ministers goes to the altar, places the Host into the monstrance, puts the monstrance in the centre of the corporal facing the people, genuflects and returns to his/her place. At the chair the president stands for the Prayer after Communion (TS: p. 519). If a congregational prayer is also used, 'You have opened to us the Scriptures, O Christ' (CWMV: p. 297), with its reference to being blessed by Christ's royal presence and walking with him until we behold him in the glory of the eternal Trinity, is particularly appropriate.

After the prayer(s) the president may change the chasuble for a white cope. The crucifer and acolytes (with lanterns rather than torches) form up as they would normally do at the end of the

Eucharist, leaving enough space for the thurifer(s) and ministers to come between them and the altar. At the same time the ministers approach the altar, genuflect and kneel. *O Salutaris Hostia* (NEH 269, vv. 5–6) or verses from another Eucharistic hymn are sung. As soon as the hymn starts, the ministers stand and the president puts incense into the thurible(s). One of the assistant ministers may take the incense boat while the other holds back one side of the cope. Although it used to be customary for incense not to be blessed in the presence of the Blessed Sacrament (see, for example, Fortescue and O'Connell 1948: p. 246) it is now suggested that incense should be blessed whenever it is imposed (Elliott 1995: p. 681). Kneeling again, the ministers bow; taking one of the thuribles, the president censes the sacrament with three double swings. The ministers bow again and the thurible is returned to the thurifer. The thurifer(s) then move to stand east of the acolytes and crucifer. If a humeral veil is used, a server places it round the president's shoulders. As soon as it has been secured, the ministers stand and approach the altar. After genuflecting, one of the ministers gives the monstrance to the president so that the president's hands are covered by the humeral veil. The ministers then turn and the procession begins.

The order of procession is similar to that on Maundy Thursday, except that suitable banners (Elliott suggests not those of Mary or the saints: Elliott 1995: p. 257) may be carried and a Eucharistic banner may replace the processional cross. The order is as follows: the acolytes, crucifer (or banner bearer) and children with rose petals are followed by any ministers who are not assisting the president, the thurifer(s), the president holding the monstrance (with a minister either side, possibly holding back the cope and, if the monstrance is heavy, supporting the president's elbows). If a canopy is used, it is carried by members of the congregation and held above the monstrance; and up to six torch bearers (servers or members of the congregation) may surround it. The choir, if there is one, and the congregation with their hand-held candles follow the president. If there are additional servers, they may be dispersed among the congregation carrying banners or, alternatively, follow the cross and lights. An MC can fulfil a useful role in marshalling the procession. He or she can control the pace and also ring bells to indicate the presence of the Sacrament. Eucharistic hymns and chants should be sung throughout the procession, both inside and outside the church.

The music should be carefully chosen so as to make the procession an occasion for joy and celebration. If the route is long, Benediction may be given at selected points along the way (Elliott 1995: p. 258).

At the end of the procession the ministers approach the altar. The president, assisted by one of the ministers, places the monstrance on the altar, and all genuflect. If the procession has returned to the same church where the Eucharist was celebrated, additional candles and flowers may be placed on the altar while the procession is outside. An altar in another church may be similarly decorated. If a throne has been placed in the centre of the altar, an assistant minister places the monstrance on it for the period of adoration which follows. The president and people kneel in the presence of the Sacrament and the humeral veil is removed.

If the rite is to conclude with Benediction, the president or another minister may first lead a short act of devotion, which could include the acclamation included in TS (p. 520). After a period of silence the *Tantum ergo* (NEH 268, vv. 5–6) or verses from another suitable hymn are sung. Incense is imposed in the same way as at the beginning of the procession and the Sacrament is censed with three double swings.

The following response may be used:

| | |
|---|---|
| *President* | You gave them bread from heaven. Alleluia. |
| *All* | **Containing in itself all sweetness. Alleluia.** |

before the president sings 'Let us pray' and then stands to sing the collect. If the CW collect (TS: p. 515) has been used during the Gathering, another suitable prayer should be used here, such as:

> Lord, give to our hearts
> the light of faith and the fire of love,
> that we may worship in spirit and in truth
> our Lord and God, present in this sacrament,
> who lives and reigns for ever and ever.
> (Adapted from *The Rites* 1990: p. 697)

Alternatively another collect, such as one of the ICEL texts (*Opening Prayers* 1999: pp. 54–5), may be used during the Gathering and the CW collect at Benediction.

After the prayer, the president kneels again and receives the humeral veil. Standing with the assisting ministers, they approach the altar and genuflect. One of the ministers places the monstrance into the president's hands. The assistant ministers then kneel before the altar as the president turns to bless the congregation, slowly and deliberately making the sign of the cross with the monstrance. Bells may be rung and the Sacrament censed by both thuribles as Benediction is given. The organist may improvise from after the collect until the president turns to give Benediction, and then continue as the monstrance is replaced on the altar. The assistant ministers stand and genuflect with the president before all three return to their positions in front of the altar.

A form of the Divine Praises may follow and/or the service may conclude with a hymn, chant or acclamation of thanksgiving. During the hymn one of the assistant ministers approaches the altar, genuflects, removes the Sacrament, places it in a pyx and takes it to wherever the Sacrament is reserved. The monstrance may be placed next to the corporal, sideways on, and covered with a white veil. A bell is rung to signify that the Sacrament has been placed in the tabernacle or aumbry and as a signal for all to stand. The ministers and servers who are not carrying anything reverence the altar with a bow or genuflection (if the Sacrament is reserved there) before processing out in the usual way.

# The Sacred Heart of Jesus
## (Divine Compassion of Christ)

The Feast of the Sacred Heart is celebrated on the Friday following the First Sunday after Trinity. Although it has never been commemorated in an official Church of England calendar, a celebration of the Divine Compassion of Christ on this day appeared in the Franciscan publication *Celebrating Common Prayer* (1992: p. 399) and is observed in a number of Anglican places of worship, sometimes with a Sung Eucharist, as on a Sunday. The Roman Catholic Church celebrates this day as a Solemnity (with *Gloria* and Creed). White is the liturgical colour and Elliott mentions that 'in some places the charity of Christ is reflected in special collections of money, food and clothing for the poor, which may be incorporated into the procession of gifts' (Elliott 2002: p. 172).

There is much to commend this celebration. Where it is observed, the following liturgical material, taken from CW, *Celebrating Common Prayer* and the Roman rite, may be used at the Eucharist:

## Collect

> Almighty God,
> whose Son, our Lord and Saviour Jesus Christ,
> was moved with compassion for all who had gone astray
> and with indignation for all who had suffered wrong:
> inflame our hearts with the burning fire of your love,
> that we may seek out the lost,
> have mercy on the fallen
> and stand fast for truth and righteousness;
> through Jesus Christ our Lord ...
>
> > (*Celebrating Common Prayer* 1992: p. 399)

Alternatively, one of the ICEL collects may be used (*Opening Prayers* 1999: pp. 56–7).

## Post-Communion

The CW post-Communion prayer for the weekdays after the Day of Pentecost (CWMV: p. 406) or the Sixteenth Sunday after Trinity (CWMV: p. 418) would be appropriate.

## Eucharist – Year A

Deuteronomy 7.6–11
Psalm 103.1–4, 6–8, 10
1 John 4.7–16
Matthew 11.25–30

## Eucharist – Year B

Hosea 11.1, 3–4, 8–9
Isaiah 12.2–6
Ephesians 3.8–12, 14–19
John 19.31–37

*Eucharist – Year C*

Ezekiel 34.11–16
Psalm 23
Romans 5.5–11
Luke 15.3–7

# Dedication Festival

Since at least the fourth century in many places the date on which a church building was consecrated has been celebrated as a Festival, not to be confused with the Patronal Festival of the saint to whom it is dedicated. In CW, if the actual date is not known, the Dedication may be observed on either the First Sunday in October or the Last Sunday after Trinity. If the actual date is known, then it would be preferable to observe the Dedication on that date, unless it falls in a prohibited period (Holy Week, Easter Week). TS provides a directory of material for the day in the standard categories (TS: pp. 521–7).

The precise manner of celebration will vary according to local custom – indeed, the liturgy should reflect the local, particularly if the names of the founders of the church are known, in which case they should be mentioned at least in the intercessions. The overall tone of the liturgy must be thanksgiving, and it would be appropriate to celebrate the Eucharist with greater solemnity than on an 'ordinary' Sunday. There might be a procession, perhaps around the outside of the church.

The liturgy within the church might incorporate thanksgiving for various features of the building – the font, the altar, the pulpit etc. – and their liturgical significance. This can be very effectively incorporated into a procession, but should not overload the service as a whole.

## Bible Sunday

There are no specific ceremonial aspects to Bible Sunday, but a selection of texts is provided in TS (pp. 528–34), and indeed may be used 'on any suitable occasion when the focus is on the word of God as revealed in holy Scripture (TS: p. 528, note). Where it is observed, Bible Sunday replaces the CW provision for the Last Sunday after Trinity, and the liturgical colour remains green.

## Embertide

TS provides a directory of material for use on Ember Days (pp. 636–42). This should be used appropriately in the week before a diocesan ordination and more generally on 'days of prayer for those who serve the Church in its various ministries, both ordained and lay, and for vocations' (TS: p. 636). In respect of the latter, Vocation Sunday would be an ideal opportunity to make use of this material.

# 6

# Seasons and festivals of the agricultural year

And now we give you thanks
because all things are of your making,
all times and seasons obey your laws,
but you have chosen to create us in your own image,
setting us over the whole world in its wonder.
You have made us stewards of your creation,
to praise you day by day
for the marvels of your wisdom and power.
                    (Short preface for Creation, TS: p. 603)

## Introduction

The substantial provision in TS for agricultural seasons and festivals reflects the interest in ecological and environmental issues which has grown in recent times and the concern which Christians share with peoples of other faiths and none to care for and conserve the resources of the earth.

TS sets these interests and concerns within a theological framework which combines thanksgiving with intercession and provides liturgical resources for a variety of occasions together with some helpful introductory and explanatory material.

Although there is very little that can be said in terms of ritual and ceremonial for these services, some general points can be made to encourage good practice. On these occasions a careful balance needs to be struck between focusing on the local community and the wider world. In rural communities, local farmers and agricultural workers are likely to be at the forefront of people's minds on Plough Sunday as they ask for God's blessing on them and their labours in the coming year. But such prayer should also be extended not only to farm workers in other parts of the country, but also to areas of drought, famine or crisis in the wider world. In urban communities, Harvest Thanksgiving is sometimes an opportunity for gifts to be given, such as tinned food and toiletries, to support local homelessness projects. Such an offering makes complete sense in that context, but an urban harvest festival should not exclude thanksgiving and prayer for those who produce the foods which fill the shelves of local supermarkets and shops. The theology underpinning any celebration, in whatever context, must be thanksgiving to God, the creator of heaven and earth and source of all that exists.

# Creation

TS notes that these resources may appropriately be used on the Second Sunday before Lent which, in the Church of England, has creation as its theme in all three lectionary years. Some of the material here would also be suited to a service during One World Week, for which resources can also be found on the internet at <www.oneworldweek.org>. The first of the acclamations could be used as part of the Blessing of Light at an evening service; and the second, based on verses from the book of Job, could appropriately be used at the Eucharist instead of the psalm (p. 605). Material from this section could also be used during occasional weekday services, if it is desired to include thanksgiving for creation and prayer for responsible stewardship of the earth's resources as part of a community's regular pattern of worship.

At the 2007 European Ecumenical Assembly, Roman Catholic, Orthodox, Anglican and Protestant Churches agreed that 'the period from 1 September to 4 October be dedicated to prayer for the protection of Creation and the promotion of sustainable lifestyles that reverse our contribution to climate change'. In many churches a Sunday Harvest Festival will provide the focus for such prayer and, perhaps also the Feast of St Francis of Assisi (4 October). Material from the creation section of TS is also well suited to this period. Further resources can be also be found on the Church of England Liturgical Commission's website, <www.transformingworship. org.uk>, as well as that of Churches Together in Britain and Ireland, <www.ctbi.org.uk>.

## Plough Sunday

Plough Sunday may be observed on the First Sunday of Epiphany, which is also the Festival of the Baptism of Christ. TS provides rich liturgical resources for the latter, so care must be taken not to overload the worship on this day. However, if a plough and/or seed are to be blessed, this could happen informally before the blessing and dismissal, instead of the dismissal Gospel (TS: p. 182), or after the service has finished. It would be appropriate for the priest to say the prayers of blessing with hands in the *orans* position, making the sign of the cross at the words 'By your blessing'. After the end of their respective prayers, the plough and seed could be sprinkled with water taken from the font.

## Rogation

TS provides material for the Eucharist at Rogationtide (the Sunday and days leading up to Ascension Day) (TS: pp. 609–13), and specifically for a Rogationtide procession (pp. 614–18). Rogation Sunday is an ideal opportunity to 'beat the bounds' of the parish where this is practicable. If this is to take place, various stations may be made around the boundaries of the parish, with appropriate prayers. Thus the beating of the bounds may form part of a Rogationtide procession, but should not be done more than once a year.

The Rogation procession may occur inside the church, but should be done outside if at all possible according to the character and geography of the parish, for example along lanes and field paths in rural areas. The opportunity such a procession presents for an urban or rural public act of witness should not be lost: in the countryside it might form part of a extended day out for the whole community including children's activities, a picnic lunch, perhaps receiving hospitality at farms and houses along the route, and concluding with Evensong back in church. George Herbert's approving words about such outdoor parish processions to which we referred in Chapter 1 of ALG 5 (p. 20) are especially relevant here.

## Lammastide

TS provides some background to the celebration of Lammas Day, suggesting that it originated as an English festival celebrated on 1 August in thanksgiving for the first-fruits of the wheat harvest (p. 598). In the middle of the last century the Anglican liturgist, Gregory Dix, was asked to comment on the origins of this Festival and declared that it was not English at all but 'of Italian origin', going on to say that

> The emphasis laid on this aspect of 1st August by some modern Anglican liturgists seems to be a modern invention, not based on authentic tradition at all.
>
> (Jones 2007: pp. 34–5)

Whatever the provenance of this day, in some communities it will be appropriate to give thanks for the first-fruits of the harvest and so, as TS suggests, it would make sense for Lammastide to coincide with this rather than being fixed at the beginning of August. The presentation of the Lammas loaf, preferably made with flour from the first grains of the harvest, has the potential for rich Eucharistic associations, particularly if the second set of readings is chosen (TS: p. 621). It would therefore be appropriate for a portion of the Lammas loaf to be used as the bread for the Eucharist, even if it is the normal custom to use wafer-bread.

TS provides a fully worked out form of the Gathering at the Eucharist which includes the presentation of the Lammas loaf. If possible, the loaf should be brought to the president by some of those involved in the harvest and the person who has baked it. If part of the loaf is to be used for the Eucharist, a portion should be cut from it at the offertory. The rest could be shared by members of the congregation after the service.

## Harvest Thanksgiving

In the past 'Harvest Festival', one of the most popular occasions in the Christian year, has often been prone to a lack of properly liturgical structure. The material for Harvest Thanksgiving in TS (pp. 623–32) goes a long way towards remedying this, without excluding local custom and imagination. The material clearly has the Eucharist mainly in view, but several elements (confession, intercession, etc.) could easily be included in a non-Eucharistic service and would contribute towards a clear structure. While the TS resources are included among those for Seasons and Festivals of the Agricultural Year, urban communities should not dismiss the possibilities for adaptation to that setting, bearing in mind that food in the supermarkets has to come from somewhere! The need to pray for and give thanks for the fruits of the earth and the sea is universal. Whatever the community, the liturgical vision should be also to the wider world, particularly those places where the growing and supplying of food is precarious, and this is reflected in the TS material.

It is customary for the church to be decorated for Harvest Thanksgiving. This need not be excessive, as Percy Dearmer emphasized in saying that 'Harvest Festivals have been much abused by excessive displays of greengrocery' (Dearmer 1932: p. 469); but the decoration ought certainly to reflect the community in which the church is set. Items should not be placed on the altar itself – the focus there must remain the bread and wine of the Eucharist.

If the Harvest Thanksgiving is to take place at the Sunday Eucharist, the CW Lectionary provides readings for all three years which may be substituted for those of the ordinary Sunday. It is appropriate for the liturgical colour to remain that of Ordinary Time (green), although some communities may possess special vestments and textile hangings for the occasion.

TS includes material written specifically for an act of thanksgiving (p. 625) and the Bringing Forward of Symbols of the Harvest (p. 629). The former should not be taken to be an alternative to the Intercessions (TS: pp. 626–8). The liturgy of the Bringing Forward of Symbols is an opportunity to involve members of the community of all ages. The symbols might well include various items grown or made (for example loaves) by members of the community, and may be placed around, but not on, the altar. The rite can appropriately take place after the Peace and immediately before the Preparation of the Table. The presenting of the bread and wine can be incorporated into the form, the president placing them upon the altar in the usual way in readiness for the Eucharistic Prayer, and praising God for these gifts of creation using the TS Prayer at the Preparation of the Table (p. 630). Then the hymn verse 'Praise God, from whom all blessings flow' (TS: p. 629) can be sung before the Eucharistic Prayer begins. Thus:

- Peace.
- Harvest hymn begins.
- Bringing Forward of Symbols.
- Presentation of bread and wine.
- Preparation of the altar.
- Thanksgivings for each symbol.
- Prayer at the preparation of the table.
- 'Praise God, from whom all blessings flow', etc.
- Eucharistic Prayer.

If this adapted order is followed, the offertory hymn should be omitted, although a suitable Harvest hymn may appropriately be sung before or during the Bringing Forward, the words accompanying each symbol being said in sequence when those bringing the symbols have all arrived at the sanctuary and the hymn has finished.

## Agricultural crisis

Recent crises in the farming industry have brought home to all the precarious nature of the harvest and of animal husbandry, even in the developed world. Two prayers are provided in TS for use at such times (p. 633).

# Sources

## Texts and resources

Ambrose, G., *Together for a Season: All-Age Seasonal Resources for Lent, Holy Week and Easter* (London: Church House Publishing, 2007).

Benedict XVI, *Way of the Cross* (London: Burns & Oates, 2005).

*The Book of Occasional Services*, The Episcopal Church (New York: The Church Hymnal Corporation, 2004).

Breighner, J., *Beyond Easter Sunday: Stations of the Resurrection* (New London, CT: Twenty-Third Publications, 2002).

*Celebrating Common Prayer* (London: Mowbray, 1992).

*Celebrating the Easter Mystery: Worship Resources for Easter to Pentecost*, ed. Christopher Irvine (London: Mowbray, 1996).

Chapman, R., *Stations of the Resurrection* (Norwich: Canterbury Press, 1998).

*Common Praise* (Norwich: Canterbury Press, 2000).

*Common Worship: Christian Initiation* (London: Church House Publishing, 2006).

*Common Worship: Daily Eucharistic Lectionary*, ed. S. Kershaw (Norwich: Canterbury Press, 2008).

*Common Worship: Daily Prayer* (London: Church House Publishing, 2005).

*Common Worship: Festivals* (London: Church House Publishing, 2007).

*Common Worship: Pastoral Services* (London: Church House Publishing, 2000).

*Common Worship: Proclaiming the Passion* (London: Church House Publishing, 2007).

*Common Worship: Services and Prayers for the Church of England* (London: Church House Publishing, 2000).

*Common Worship: Services and Prayers for the Church of England: President's Edition* (London: Church House Publishing, 2000).

*Common Worship: Times and Seasons* (London: Church House Publishing, 2006).

*The English Hymnal* (London: Oxford University Press, 1933).

*The English Missal,* reprint (Norwich: Canterbury Press, 2002).

*Enriching the Christian Year,* ed. Michael Perham et al. (London: SPCK/Alcuin Club, 1993).

*Enriching the Liturgy,* ed. J. P. Young (London: SPCK, 1998).

Griffiths, Alan, *Celebrating the Christian Year – Volume II: Lent, Holy Week & Easter* (Norwich: Canterbury Press, 2005).

Irvine, Christopher, ed., *The Use of Symbols in Worship,* Alcuin Liturgy Guides 4 (London: SPCK, 2007).

*Lent, Holy Week, Easter: Services and Prayers* (London: CHP/CUP/ SPCK, 1986).

*The Methodist Worship Book* (Peterborough: Methodist Publishing House, 1999).

Milner-White, E., *A Procession of Passion Prayers* (London: SPCK, 1956).

*The New English Hymnal* (Norwich: Canterbury Press, 1986).

*New Patterns for Worship* (London: Church House Publishing, 2002).

*Opening Prayers: Scripture-related Collects for Years A, B & C from The Sacramentary,* The ICEL Collects, ICEL (Norwich: Canterbury Press, 1999).

Peterson, John, *A Walk in Jerusalem: Stations of the Cross* (Harrisburg, PA: Morehouse Publishing, 1998).

Plainsong and Medieval Music Society, *Compline: An Order for Night Prayer in Traditional Language* (Dorking: RSCM Press, 2005).

Royal School of Church Music, *Music for Common Worship VI: Night Prayer (Compline)* (Dorking: RSCM Press, 2005).

*The Sacramentary* (New York: Catholic Book Publishing Co., 1985).

*The Sunday Missal* (London: HarperCollins, 2005).

Vanstone, W. H., *Icons of the Passion: A Way of the Cross,* 2nd edition (London: Darton, Longman & Todd, 2000).

von Balthasar, Hans Urs, *The Way of the Cross* (Slough: St Paul Publications, 1990).

*The Walsingham Pilgrim Manual* (Walsingham College Trust Association, many editions).

*The Weekday Missal* (London: Collins, 1982).

## Studies, guides and other works

*Anglican Services: A Book Concerning Ritual and Ceremonial in the Church of England* (London: W. Knott & Son, 1953).

Bradshaw, Paul, ed., *Companion to Common Worship Vol. 1,* Alcuin Club Collections 78 (London: SPCK, 2001).

Bradshaw, Paul, ed., *Companion to Common Worship Vol. 2,* Alcuin Club Collections 81 (London: SPCK, 2006).

Dean, Stephen, ed., *The Great Week* (McCrimmons, 1992).

Dearmer, Percy, *The Parson's Handbook*, 12th edition (London: Oxford University Press, 1932).

*A Directory of Ceremonial*, Part II, Alcuin Club Tracts XIX, second edition (London: Mowbray, 1950).

Elliott, Peter J., *Ceremonies of the Liturgical Year According to the Modern Roman Rite* (San Francisco: Ignatius Press, 2002).

Elliott, Peter J., *Ceremonies of the Modern Roman Rite* (San Francisco: Ignatius Press, 1995).

*Eucharistic Presidency: A Theological Statement by the House of Bishops of the General Synod* (London: Church House Publishing, 1997).

Foley, E., Mitchell, N. D. and Pierce, J. M., eds, *A Commentary on the General Instruction of the Roman Missal* (Collegeville, MN: Liturgical Press, 2007).

Fortescue, Adrian and O'Connell, J., *The Ceremonies of the Roman Rite Described*, 8th edition further revised (London: Burns Oates and Washbourne, 1948).

Galley, Howard E, *The Ceremonies of the Eucharist: A Guide to Celebration* (Cambridge, MA: Cowley Publications, 1989).

*General Instruction of the Roman Missal* (London: Catholic Truth Society, 2005).

Giles, Richard, *Times and Seasons: Creating Transformative Worship Throughout the Year* (Norwich: Canterbury Press, 2008).

Gordon-Taylor, B. and Jones, S., *Celebrating Christ's Appearing: Advent to Candlemas*, Alcuin Liturgy Guides 5 (London: Alcuin Club/ SPCK, 2008).

Gordon-Taylor, B. and Jones, S., *Celebrating the Eucharist*, Alcuin Liturgy Guides 3 (London: Alcuin Club/SPCK, 2005).

Greenacre, R. and Haselock, J., *The Sacrament of Easter* (Leominster: Gracewing, 1995).

Herbert, George, *The Complete English Works*, ed. A. P. Slater (London: Everyman's Library, 1995).

International Commission on English in the Liturgy, *Ceremonial of Bishops* (Collegeville: The Liturgical Press, 1989).

Irwin, Kevin W., *Lent: A Guide to the Eucharist and Hours* (New York: Pueblo, 1985).

Irwin, Kevin W., *Easter: A Guide to the Eucharist and Hours* (New York: Pueblo, 1992).

Jones, Simon, *The Sacramental Life: Gregory Dix and his Writings* (Norwich: Canterbury Press, 2007).

Kennedy, D. and Haselock, L., *Using Common Worship Times and Seasons, Vol. 2* (London: Church House Publishing, 2008).

Larkin, P., ed., *The Oxford Book of Twentieth-Century English Verse* (Oxford: Clarendon Press, 1973).

MacGregor, A. J., *Fire and Light in the Western Triduum: Their Use at Tenebrae and at the Paschal Vigil* (Collegeville, MN: Liturgical Press, 1992).

Michno, D., *A Priest's Handbook: The Ceremonies of the Church* (New York: Morehouse, 1998).

Monti, James, *The Week of Salvation: History and Traditions of Holy Week* (Huntington, IN: Our Sunday Visitor, 1993).

Perham, Michael and Stevenson, Kenneth, *Waiting for the Risen Christ: A Commentary on Lent, Holy Week, Easter: Services and Prayers* (London: SPCK, 1986).

*The Rites of the Catholic Church: Volume 1* (New York: Pueblo, 1990).

*Ritual Notes* (London: W. Knott & Son, 1946, 1947 and 1956).

Stevenson, Kenneth, *All the Company of Heaven: A Companion to the Principal Festivals of the Christian Year* (Norwich: Canterbury Press, 1998).

Talley, Thomas, *The Origins of the Liturgical Year* (New York: Pueblo, 1986).

Toal, M. F., *The Sunday Sermons of the Great Fathers*, Vol. 3 (London: Longmans, 1959).

Wilkinson, John, *Egeria's Travels* (Warminster: Arris & Phillips, 1999).

Wright, Geoffrey, *Living Traditions* (London: Church Union, 1994).

Yarnold, Edward, ed., *The Awe-Inspiring Rites of Initiation* (Edinburgh: T&T Clark, 1994).

# Index